GOSPEL OFFENSE

ADVANCING GOD'S KINGDOM WITH LOVE

BRIAN BENTON

WESTBOW
PRESS®
A DIVISION OF THOMAS NELSON
& ZONDERVAN

WestBow Press books may be ordered through booksellers or by contacting:

WestBow Press
A Division of Thomas Nelson & Zondervan
1663 Liberty Drive
Bloomington, IN 47403
www.westbowpress.com
844-714-3454

Unless otherwise indicated, all Scripture quotations taken from the (NASB®) New American Standard Bible®, Copyright © 1960, 1971, 1977, 1995, 2020 by The Lockman Foundation. Used by permission. All rights reserved. www.lockman.org

Scripture quotations marked (NLT) are taken from the Holy Bible, New Living Translation, copyright ©1996, 2004, 2015 by Tyndale House Foundation. Used by permission of Tyndale House Publishers, Carol Stream, Illinois 60188. All rights reserved.

Acknowledgement Edited by Jennifer Legate

ISBN: 978-1-6642-4636-2 (sc)
ISBN: 978-1-6642-4637-9 (e)

Library of Congress Control Number: 2021920591

Print information available on the last page.

WestBow Press rev. date: 10/20/2021

CONTENTS

ABOUT THE AUTHOR

Brian Benton is a Jesus follower, husband, father, friend, author, and entrepreneur. He is passionate about reaching people with the Gospel to multiply the Kingdom of God and to inspire people to reach their God-given potential.

He is a high school drop out that graduated cum laude from Middle Tennessee State University with a Bachelor of Science Degree in 2011 at the age of 31. He founded his first IT business, Xccelero, in 2013 without any outside capital or loans after working in the IT field for 13 years.

He is the author of *The Hurry Up No Huddle Life Offense; Business Offense: How to Win with People, Process, and Technology; The Business Offense Playbook; and ITOS: How to Accelerate Business with the Information Technology Offense System.*

Brian has served as a middle school youth pastor, life group leader, and Awana group co-leader.

INTRODUCTION

I started writing this book in 2020 during a presidential election year with a global pandemic, economic uncertainty, racial tensions, and political divisions. There was a lot of fear, deception, half-truths, spin, unrest, anxiety, and depression. It was a time when people of faith were limited how they could worship inside the walls of the church in a country founded on freedom of religion. It was a time where the United States and other nations were humbled by a virus. It was a time where government leaders of all countries seized the opportunity to tighten their grip of power over their respective populations. In short, it was a time of a lot of bad news and focus on COVID 19 deaths. Regardless of bad news, now or in the future, there is always the Good News of the Gospel of Jesus Christ.

DEDICATION

To all the men and women who have served in our armed forces: Thank you for your sacrifice and keeping our nation free.

To all the family members of men and women who have served in our armed forces: Thank you for your sacrifice and allowing the men and women in your life to keep our nation free.

To all my family members, friends, pastors, mentors, clients, and former bosses: Thank you for your love, support, encouragement, and wisdom.

SECTION I
Gospel Attack

The Outbreak of War

At the beginning of the 20th century, the German, Austria-Hungary, and Ottoman Empires fought against Great Britain, the United States, France, Russia, Italy, and Japan. The war became known as World War I and was deemed "the war to end all wars." Unfortunately "the war to end all wars" led to the deaths of over 16 million people, caused instability in Europe, and set the stage for the rise of the Nazi party in Germany.

The leader of the Nazi party, Adolf Hitler, rearmed Germany and signed treaties with Japan and Italy. Hitler's ultimate plan was to dominate the world and kill all the Jews. In 1939, Hitler invaded Poland, thus starting World War II. Germany, Italy, and Japan—known as the Axis powers—fought against Great Britain, France, the United States, and Russia—known as the Allied powers.

Over the next six years, approximately 45 million people were killed, and 6 million Jews were murdered. From an American perspective, the Axis powers were the bad guys and from the Axis powers' perspective the Allied powers were the bad guys. So who were the "good guys" and who were the "bad guys" in World War II? The answer will vary depending on your perspective and worldview. The next question is: If there is good and evil in the world, where or who does good and evil come from? My worldview of good and evil comes directly from the Bible.

In Genesis 1:1-25, God created the heavens and the earth. He started each command with the word "Let..." Then in Genesis

1:26-31, He created man in His image and likeness saying, "Let Us make mankind." The words "Let Us" refer to God existing as three persons: Father, Son, and Holy Spirit—known as the Trinity. The word trinity is not in the Bible, but the revelation of the Trinity is throughout the Bible.

The most common reference to the Trinity is the baptism of Jesus recorded in the Gospels. As Jesus was baptized, the Father declared, "This is my beloved Son, in whom I am well pleased." Then a dove, symbolizing the Holy Spirit, descended from heaven (Luke 3:21-22). As God the Father, God the Son, and God the Spirit created the various parts of the physical world, He paused to see that what He had created was good. The reason it was good is because God is good. So if God is good and created a good world, then why is there evil in the world?

Sometime in eternity past, war broke out in heaven when a powerful angel, Satan, rebelled against God, which led to the first act of evil in the universe. The Bible doesn't provide details about the creation of angels, but it does reveal that three types of angels exist: Cherubim (Genesis 3:24, Exodus 25:22, Ezekiel 10:1-22, Psalm 18:10), Seraphim (Isaiah 6:2-7), and Living Creatures (Ezekiel 1:5-14, Revelation 4:6-8).

Scripture also reveals God delegated different roles and responsibilities to angels: praise and worship (Isaiah 6:3), communication (Luke 1:26-56), warfare (2 Samuel 24:16), protection (Psalm 34:7, Psalm 91:11), provision (Matthew 4:11), and destruction (Genesis 19:1-13).

One of the most popular stories in the Bible where angels are sent by God to destroy something is in Genesis 19. God sent two angels to rescue Lot and his family. Then they destroyed Sodom and Gomorrah for their sin against God. One of the least spoken about passages in the Bible is found in 2 Samuel 24:1-17. King David built a powerful army including "mighty men", which we would refer to in the modern era as elite special forces.

David decided to count his men, which to God was an act of

pride because it wasn't David winning the battles, it was God winning the battles. David's top commander, Joab, warned David not to count his men, but David, incited by Satan and rooted in pride, had his entire army counted. God disapproved of David counting his men so much that he presented David with three choices of discipline.

David chose the shortest one, and God sent an angel to kill 70,000 of David's people. As the angel was about to destroy Jerusalem with a sword, God demonstrated mercy by commanding the angel to stop the attack. God only needed to send one angel to kill 70,000 men. Angels are very powerful compared to humans!

In Jude 1:6, Daniel 10:13, and Revelation 12:7 we learn there is a chain of command in the angelic ranks. Michael is referred to as the Archangel in Jude 1:9 and is mentioned in Daniel 10:13 and Revelation 12:7. Each mention of his name in these chapters is related to warfare. In Revelation 12:7, the Scripture states, "Michael and his angels fought", which indicates he and his angels engaged in warfare.

In Jude 1:6, Scripture reveals there are angels that left their "own domain", which indicates God delegated responsibility to angels to operate over certain domains in His creation. The Scripture doesn't reveal what those domains are, but these angels obviously disobeyed God because they will be punished for eternity. The most important difference between angels and humans is that humans have an opportunity to repent, whereas angels do not have that opportunity.   Some   theologians believe Ezekiel 28 and Isaiah 14 point to the fall of Satan. I'm not exactly sure if these passages point to the fall of Satan, but I'm exactly sure of what Jesus said in Luke 10:18, "I was watching Satan fall from heaven like lightning." Whatever Satan did in heaven, he was kicked out at the speed of light. Satan is so clever and deceptive that he convinced one third of the angels to follow him and rebel against God in the presence of God, as indicated in Revelation 12:4, "And his tail swept away a third of the stars of heaven and hurled them to the earth." The term "stars" in this passage refers to angels.

In Revelation 12:9 we are provided more details of their fall: "And the great dragon was thrown down, the serpent of old who is called the devil and Satan, who deceives the whole world; he was thrown down to the earth, and his angels were thrown down with him."

If Satan can convince one third of the angels in heaven to rebel against God in His presence, how easy is it for him to influence humans who already are in a state of rebellion against God?

GOSPEL ATTACK: CHAPTER 2

Defeat of the First Man

In the creation account of Genesis, God spoke everything into existence except for man. In the creation account of man, God said "Let Us make mankind in Our image, according to Our likeness..." (Genesis 1:26). The words "Let Us" refer to the Father, Son, and Holy Spirit agreeing on their plan to create mankind. The words "make mankind in Our image, according to Our likeness" are explained in Genesis 2:7: "Then the Lord God formed the man of dust from the ground, and breathed into his nostrils the breath of life; and the man became a living person."

In other words, God handcrafted the first man into existence like a potter forms clay and then breathed breath into his nostrils. God gave man life so that he would worship and glorify Him while ruling over the earth.

One of the first assignments God gave Adam was to name every animal, which probably took a considerable amount of time. Then after Adam named every animal, God said in Genesis 2:18, "It is not good for the man to be alone; I will make him a helper suitable for him." God loved Adam so much that he was saving the best for last. God put Adam into a deep sleep, took a rib from his body, and made woman.

When Adam woke up from the deep sleep he saw a naked woman in front of him for the first time. Remember, they're in the Garden of Eden with no curse, no kids, no neighbors, no problems and....God had already commanded Adam to be fruitful and multiply. How long do you think Adam waited until he obeyed that command? I suspect he had blood flow if you know what I mean and didn't wait very long. I don't know about you, but I would love for God to place me in a garden with my wife with no curse, no kids, no neighbors, and no problems so that we can be fruitful and multiply. However, I'm sure I would find some way to mess it up just like Adam did.

God instructed Adam and Eve they could eat from any tree of the garden except for the tree of the knowledge of good and evil. God placed this special tree in the middle of the garden so Adam and Eve would know exactly which tree God was referring to. God said if you touch or eat from the tree of the knowledge of good and evil you will surely die. So why did God create the tree of the knowledge of good and evil and place it in the middle of the Garden of Eden? God created Adam with the ability to choose to love Him, which is obeying God. First John 5:3 says, "For this is the love of God, that we keep His commandments; and His commandments are not burdensome."

Satan Declares War on Man

Pastor Judah Smith preached a message where he describes how God "stacked the system" in Adam and Eve's favor for them not to sin in the Garden of Eden. After reading through the Genesis account many times, I agree that God did "stack the system" in Adam and Eve's favor. God did not want them to give in to sin.

He wanted a relationship with them. He wanted them to remain innocent and only know good. He wanted them to remain close to Him and be obedient to Him out of love for Him. He wanted them to care for and cultivate His garden for His glory. However, the chief enemy of God, Satan, had been cast down to Earth and was in the garden. He hated God and His creation. Satan was listening when God told Adam he could freely eat the fruit from all the trees but couldn't touch or eat from the tree of the knowledge of good and evil.

Satan waited until Eve was created, then he unleashed his first attack against man. Satan asked Eve in Genesis 3:1, "Has God really said, 'You shall not eat from any tree of the garden'?" Eve replied in Genesis 3:2-3, "From the fruit of the trees of the garden we may eat; but from the fruit of the tree which is in the middle of the garden, God has said, 'You shall not eat from it or touch it, or you will die.'"

The serpent said to the woman in Genesis 3:4-6, "You certainly will not die! For God knows that on the day you eat from it your eyes will be opened, and you will become like God, knowing good and evil." When the woman saw that the tree was good for food, and that it was a delight to the eyes, and that the tree was desirable to make one wise, she took some of its fruit and ate; and she also gave some to her husband with her, and he ate."

According to 1 John 2:16, there are three ways humans are tempted: the lust of the eyes, the lust of the flesh, and the pride of life. Satan influenced Eve to focus on the fruit with her eyes (lust of the eyes) because it was desirable for her body (lust of the flesh) and it would make her wise like God (pride of life). Adam was with her and didn't do anything to stop the serpent because he gave into the same temptation as Eve.

Man Declares War Against God

Although the system in the garden favored Adam and Eve not to sin, both Adam and Eve still gave into sin. After they ate the fruit, they became self-aware of their nakedness and experienced shame because they had disobeyed God. They tried to hide and cover up their sin with fig leaves, but God knew exactly where they were. God walked up to them in the "cool of the day" (Genesis 3:8) to demonstrate to us that He makes the first move to reconcile and restore our relationship with Him.

God asked Adam if he had eaten the fruit from the tree. Adam immediately started blaming God because He had created Eve, who influenced him to eat the fruit. Ultimately, Adam declared his independence from God by not loving God, not loving himself, and not loving his neighbor. This act of independence is a nice way of saying Adam declared war against God.

The bad news is that this act of war led to man becoming spiritually dead with no hope of overcoming sin or escaping death. The entire earth became cursed, and Satan became the god of this planet. The good news is God showed us a glimpse of His plans to offer peace terms and reconciliation for man in Genesis 3. God made the first move by walking towards Adam and Eve after they had sinned. Then God covered Adam and Eve with garments of animal skin. Scripture doesn't say how He made the garments, but I believe it was God who killed an animal, skinned the animal, and then clothed Adam and Eve with the skins of the animal as a picture of His grace that would cover our sins by the blood of Jesus.

In the old covenant, God required man to atone for their sins by the blood of an animal (Leviticus 17:11) as a foreshadow of Jesus, the Lamb of God, paying the ultimate sacrifice with His blood (Romans 5:9) for the sins of everyone who believes (Acts 13:39).

God foreknew man and Satan would rebel against Him, but His plans cannot be thwarted. He pre-planned defeating evil from the beginning of time as well as pre-planned rescuing mankind from death. A great story in the Bible of how God's plan cannot be thwarted is found in the book of Job.

God's Plans Cannot Be Thwarted

The book of Job is the oldest book in the Bible, although it's located towards the middle of the Old Testament. In the first chapter we learn Job was considered righteous, upright, and blameless in the sight of God. He was a wealthy man who was blessed by God. He feared God and turned away from evil. God had placed a hedge of protection around Job, blessed the works of his hands, and increased his possessions. Job had no idea that God was going to remove His hedge of protection and allow Satan, the adversary of God and man, to attack him and his family.

In Job 1:6-7, the sons of God presented themselves before the Lord, and Satan also appeared with them. We don't know exactly who the sons of God are, but we do know Satan came with them. The Lord asked Satan, "From where do you come?" and Satan answered the Lord, "From roaming about on the earth and walking around on it." The reason Satan was roaming about on the earth and walking around on it was because he was "looking for someone to devour" (1 Peter 5:8).

In Job 1:8 the Lord said to Satan, "Have you considered My servant Job?" Then the Lord praised Job saying, "For there is no one like him on the earth, a blameless and upright man, fearing God and turning away from evil." In Job 1:9-12, Satan immediately accuses Job of only fearing God because of God's protection, blessings, and provisions. Satan declares to God that if He touches all Job has, Job will surely curse God to His face. Then the Lord grants Satan permission to attack Job. Yes, God gave Satan, who by his nature is evil, permission to attack Job's family and possessions.

In Job 1:13-22, Satan unleashes a vicious and merciless attack in the form of the Sabeans, the Chaldeans, fire, and wind that killed Job's family members and destroyed his possessions. At the end of Chapter 1, Job falls to the ground to worship God and never sins or blames God. He declares that the Lord gave and the Lord has taken away.

In Job 2:1, Satan comes before the Lord on the same day the sons of God present themselves before the Lord. There seems to be an appointed time God allows the sons of God to present themselves and Satan knows that appointed time, so he tags along. The Lord asks Satan in Job 2:2, "Where have you come from?" Then Satan answers the Lord and says, "From roaming about on the earth and walking around on it."

In Job 2:3, "The Lord said to Satan, "Have you considered My servant Job?" The Lord praises Job saying in Job 2:3, "For there is no one like him on the earth, a blameless and upright man fearing God and turning away from evil. And he still holds his integrity, although you incited Me against him to ruin him without cause." Then Satan responds to God in Job 2:4-5, "Skin for skin! Yes, all that a man has, he will give for his life. However, put forth Your hand now, and touch his bone and his flesh; he will curse You to Your face."

In Job 2:6-10, the Lord granted Satan permission to attack Job but said he must spare his life. Satan smote Job—aka tortured Job—with severe boils all over his body. According to WebMD.com, a boil is caused by a bacterial skin infection. The boils were so bothersome for Job that he scraped them off with a potsherd, which is basically a broken piece of a pot. His wife was unkind to him and told him to curse God and die, yet Job didn't sin with his lips.

In Job 2:11-13, Job's three friends, Eliphaz, Bildad, and Zophar visit him to comfort and sympathize with him, but they were unable to recognize him from a distance. They sat down with him for seven days and seven nights without speaking a word because Job was in great pain. In Job 3:1, Job curses the day he was born but doesn't curse God, unlike what Satan predicted would happen.

In Job Chapters 4-37, we learn Eliphaz, Bildad, and Zophar do not speak what is right about God and are no help to Job. Job reveals a lot in these chapters: God is just, Job's life seems futile, there is no arbitrator between God and Man, Job despairs over God's dealings, Job chides his accusers, he believes in the power of God, he believes he will be vindicated, he knows he will die, he believes God shattered him, he became a byword, he believes his Redeemer lives, he believes God will deal with the wicked, he longs for God, he believes God ignores wrongs, he reaffirms his righteousness, he remembers his past was glorious, his present state is humiliating, he asserts his integrity.

In Job Chapters 38-41, God speaks to Job and questions him. God declares who He is, His mighty power, His creative power, His details of creation, His power shown in creation, and His sovereignty over everything. In Job 42:5, Job confesses to God, "I have heard of you by the hearing of the ear; but now my eye sees You; therefore I retract, and I repent in dust and ashes." In this moment, I believe Job drew closer to God than in any other moment in his life, which is the opposite of what Satan declared to God.

In Job Chapters 1 and 2, Satan declared to God that Job would curse God to His face, or in other words, in His presence. Instead, Job praised God, admired God, humbled himself before God, and repented to God in His presence. Satan lost!

The book of Job is a great example of how God's plan cannot be thwarted because He has declared the end from the beginning. As you continue to read this book, remember God's plans cannot be thwarted. The Kingdom of God is advancing with love all over planet Earth.

SECTION 2
Gospel Offense

GOSPEL OFFENSE: CHAPTER 3

Victory through the Last Man

When you think of ancient warriors, who comes to your mind? Have you ever considered Abram in the Old Testament as a mighty warrior? If you grew up in church as a kid, you probably sung the well-known children's song "Father Abraham." Do you have that song playing in your head now?

Before Abraham became "Father Abraham", his name was Abram, and he was very close to his nephew Lot. In Genesis Chapter 14, Lot was captured during a war—a war of four kings versus five kings. The four kings defeated the five kings and took all their people and possessions. Since Lot was affiliated with the losing side, he was captured. A survivor from the war came and told Abram what happened.

Immediately after hearing what happened, Abram led his 318 trained men to pursue the four kings and their armies. He divided his forces at night, defeating them, and pursued them to Hobah. He brought back all the possessions, his nephew Lot, and also the women and the other people.

Now that you know that story, you can sing this new song with the same cadence as the original Father Abraham song: "Warrior Abram had a nephew named Lot and Lot was captured by 4 kings and those 4 kings had defeated 5 kings, so Abram gathered his 318 men, divided his forces, at night, defeated them, pursued them, rescued Lot, with his possessions, and also the women, and the other people.....God wins....the end!"

The story of Abram rescuing Lot foreshadows how Jesus, The Great Warrior King, left heaven to come to the earth to rescue mankind from the dominion of darkness (Colossians 1:13).

Heaven Invades the Earth

God allowed sin and death to enter through the disobedience of the first man, Adam (Romans 5:12), so that as the last man, Jesus (1 Corinthians 15:45), He would defeat sin and death. Jesus, the Son of God, humbled Himself, taking on the form of a bond-servant (Philippians 2:7) and surrendered to the will of the Father (Mark 14:36) to come to the earth filled with enemies of God (Romans 5:10). He came to the earth knowing that His purpose was to become the final atonement of sin (2 Corinthians 5:21) and to experience death on a cross (Matthew 27:11-50). He came knowing the opposition was great and that most people would reject Him. He was driven by the love of God (John 3:16) to win people with the love of God.

Jesus was born of the virgin Mary, conceived by the Holy Spirit (Matthew 1:18). He was born into a family of carpenters (Mark 6:3), but His purpose was not to build earthly buildings but to build the Kingdom of God.

In Matthew Chapter 2, Herod commanded all the firstborn to be killed shortly after Jesus was born. Herod, the king of the Jews, was allowed to rule Judea by the Romans. He wanted all firstborn to be killed because of the Old Testament prophecy of the Messiah coming to rule over the Jewish people. Herod didn't want to give up his power and misunderstood the prophecy. Jesus wasn't coming to rule over the Jewish people but to establish His rule over Jews and Gentiles of all nations in all time periods. The forces of darkness were trying to kill Jesus before he was able to start his earthly mission, but God is always one step ahead, and His plans cannot be thwarted. Herod and the forces of darkness failed at killing Jesus.

In Luke Chapter 1, John the Baptist was born at the same time as Jesus. The purpose of John the Baptist was to make ready the path of the Lord. He was the first prosperity Gospel preacher, but he didn't preach in a nice building, eat choice foods, or wear expensive clothes. As a matter of fact, he was clothed with camel hair, a leather belt, and lived on a simple diet of locusts and honey.

He appeared in the wilderness preaching a baptism of repentance for the forgiveness of sins to point people to Jesus who would baptize with the Holy Spirit (Mark 1). The Holy Spirit empowers man to be prosperous over sin, Satan, the world, and death.

As John continues his ministry, Jesus appears before him to be baptized, and John recognizes Jesus as the Lamb of God who takes away the sins of the world (John 1:28-29). When Jesus was baptized, the relationship between the Father, Son, and Holy Spirit—known as the Trinity—is revealed. The Father said, "This is my beloved son, in whom I am well pleased" (Luke 3:21-22). The Father was pleased with His son because Jesus was His son. It wasn't because of what Jesus did or what He was going to do. It was because Jesus is the Son of God.

Jesus Defeats Satan

In the Garden of Eden, God stacked the system in Adam's favor not to sin. Adam gave into temptation through the influence of Satan, which caused sin and death to enter the world. The last man, Jesus Christ, was led by the Spirit of God in the wilderness to battle Satan after fasting from food for forty days and forty nights (Matthew 4:1-2).

The King James Version of Psalm 8:5 declares, "For thou hast made him a little lower than the angels, and hast crowned him with glory and honour." Jesus, in His human nature, battled Satan, a fallen angel, thus giving Satan what appeared to be an unfair advantage, since angels are more powerful than humans. The odds of Jesus failing in His human nature were very high, but God chose the weak things of the world to shame the strong and the foolish things of the world to shame the wise (1 Corinthians 1:27).

Satan unleashed his first attack—questioning Jesus' identity as the Son of God—then tries to get Jesus to obey his command to "turn stones into bread." Satan knew Jesus was hungry and was trying to exploit his desire for food so that He might fall into the temptation of obeying Satan's command: "If You are the Son of God, command these stones become bread. He answered him and said, "It is written: 'Man shall not live on bread alone, but on every word that comes from the mouth of God'" (Matthew 4:3-4). Jesus resisted the temptation by declaring that the written Word of God is the truth.

Score: Jesus 1, Satan 0

In the second attack, Satan questions Jesus' identity again and tries to test Him by twisting Scripture: "If You are the Son of God, throw Yourself down; for it is written, 'He will command His angels concerning You'; and 'On their hands they will lift You up, so that You do not strike Your foot against a stone'" (Matthew 4:6).

Jesus said to him, "On the other hand, it is written: 'You shall not put the Lord your God to the test'" (Matthew 4:7). Jesus resisted temptation by declaring the written Word of God is the truth.

Score: Jesus 1, Satan 0

Satan doesn't question Jesus' identity during the final attack. Satan is so deceived in his own nature that he thought Jesus would worship him. "Again, the devil took Him to a very high mountain and showed Him all the kingdoms of the world and their glory; and he said to Him, "All these things I will give You, if You fall down and worship me." Then Jesus said to him,

"Go, Satan, for it is written: 'You shall worship the Lord your God, and serve Him only.'" Then the devil left Him; and behold, angels came and began to serve Him (Matthew 4:8-11). Jesus resisted the final temptation and commanded Satan to go.

Score: Jesus 1, Satan 0.

Jesus Starts His Ministry

After Jesus left the wilderness, He started His ministry preaching a message of repentance (Matthew 4:17) and started recruiting men to serve as His disciples (Matthew 4:18-22). Over the course of three years, Jesus advanced the Kingdom of God with love, transformed His twelve disciples into an elite special forces unit, and did so many amazing things "that even the world itself would not contain the books that would be written" (John 21:25).

Jesus Defeats Sin and Death

The teachings of Jesus were so offensive to the Jewish religious elite that they wanted to kill Him (John 7:1-53) because they saw Him as a threat to their power construct. Jesus called them out for faking their relationship with God and lording their power over the people (Matthew 23:1-28).

Most of the prophets in the Old Testament sent by God were killed by their own people because the people didn't want to hear what God had to say (Matthew 23:29-39). In the same way, the Jewish religious elite didn't want to hear what Jesus had to say and wanted to kill Him. The first message Jesus preached was to "Repent, for the kingdom of heaven is at hand" (Matthew 4:17). The religious elite really didn't want people to repent but rather turn to them so they could continue to be in power (Matthew 23:13).

The religious elite were trying to suppress the message of

the Gospel, just like religions and governments all over the world try to suppress the message of the Gospel today. Satan has great influence over world religions and governments (2 Corinthians 4:4). He wants to kill, steal, and destroy as many people as possible because he hates people and hates God (John 10:10).

The Jewish religious elite tried to stop Jesus many times but failed. Judas Iscariot, a disciple of Jesus, loved money more than He loved God (John 12:6) and conspired with the religious elite to kill Jesus (Luke 22:3-6). Jesus knew the whole time Judas would betray Him because He knows the beginning from the end (Revelation 22:13).

Judas led a Roman Cohort and officers from the chief priests and the Pharisees to the Garden of Gethsemane to arrest Jesus. They took Jesus to be questioned by the religious elite. The religious elite questioned Jesus, and then asked Him, "Are you the Son of God?" Jesus declared, "Yes I am!" (Luke 22:47-71)

Then the whole assembly of them took Jesus before Pilate, the Roman governor, and falsely accused Him of misleading their nation and forbidding them to pay taxes to Caesar. Pilate sent Jesus to Herod because He belonged to Herod's jurisdiction (Luke 23:1-7).

Herod, the king of the Jews under Roman authority, was overjoyed to see Jesus. Herod questioned Jesus for some time, but Jesus never answered Herod. Herod and his soldiers mocked Jesus, dressed Him in a bright shining robe, and sent Him back to Pilate (Luke 23:8-12).

Herod and Pilate concluded Jesus was innocent of the charges and would not be put to death. However, during the Jewish Passover, it was customary for Rome to release a prisoner. The religious elite insisted Pilate release Barabbas, convicted of insurrection and murder, in exchange for crucifying Jesus. The religious elite asked for a man convicted of insurrection and murder to be released, yet they had no idea their actions were an insurrection against God and that they were murdering the Son of God on a cross (Luke 23:13-25).

The Romans were very good at killing people and instilling order over civilizations. They used a wooden cross as a form of punishment to strike fear into people to obey the will of Rome. They would nail the hands and legs of people to the cross and then lift them up on the cross to be displayed publicly.

The cross symbolized Rome's power and will over the people. The cross was a symbol of shame, fear, hopelessness, and death for those punished on it. For God, the cross was an opportunity to demonstrate His great love for humanity by allowing His only Son to die in our place for our insurrection against Him. Since Adam fell into sin, man has been in a state of insurrection towards God with a sin debt that can never be repaid (Romans 5:6-21).

Pilate handed Jesus over to the Roman soldiers to be flogged, mocked, and nailed to a cross. He was lifted on a cross in the middle of two criminals hanging on their own crosses (John 19:1-18). One of the criminals hurled abuses and mocked Jesus. The other criminal rebuked the abusive criminal, admitted his crime, and proclaimed Jesus was innocent (Luke 23:39-41). He said to Jesus, "Jesus, remember me when You come into Your kingdom!" (Luke 23:42) Jesus responded immediately, "Truly I say to you, today you will be with Me in Paradise" (Luke 23:43).

We are all dead in our crimes against God with no ability to pay off our crime debt. Jesus nailed the certificate of our debt to His body on the cross so that we can receive forgiveness and be made alive together with Christ (Colossians 2:13-14). The unrepentant criminal is currently in hell and will be thrown into the lake of fire during the great white throne judgement (Revelation 20:11-15). The repentant saint is with Jesus now and forever! (Romans 6:23)

The forces of darkness, religious elite, and Roman empire thought they had eliminated a threat to their power construct by crucifying Jesus, but on the third day Jesus was resurrected from the dead (Luke 24:1-12). The resurrection of Jesus was His insurrection against the power of darkness, sin, the world, and death. The last man, Jesus, was victorious over the power of darkness, sin, the world, and death.

Jesus Commissions His Special Forces Unit

Jesus made several appearances to people after His resurrection. During His last appearance before ascending into heaven, He met with His special forces unit, the disciples, on a designated mountain in Galilee. He commissioned them to continue to advance His kingdom with these words, "All authority in heaven and on earth has been given to Me. Go therefore, and make disciples of all nations, baptizing them in the name of the Father and the Son and the Holy Spirit, teaching them to follow all that I commanded you; and behold, I am with you always, to the end of the age" (Matthew 28:18-20).

As I write this book, the special forces unit Jesus started over 2000 years ago is now a large army of disciples from all tongues, nations, and walks of life that are led by the Spirit of God to advance the Kingdom of God with love.

GOSPEL OFFENSE: CHAPTER 4

Basic Gospel Training

Initiation

I never served in the armed forces, but I have the utmost respect for the men and women who serve in the U.S. military and their families. Every branch of the military has a basic training to orientate soldiers to their general orders—how they operate, how they build military units, how the chain of command works, and how they fight. Obviously, there is a lot more to it than that, but this analogy helps give you an idea. The Kingdom of God on the earth is like a large army comprised of disciples in different branches of service from all tongues, nations, and walks of life that are led by the Spirit of God to advance the Kingdom of God with love. As the army of God, we have basic training revealed to us in the Gospels and throughout the New Testament.

The initiation process to join the army of God is simple: God first loved us → God chose us → God sent Jesus to die for our sins → God's kindness leads us to repentance → We respond to God's love and kindness by repenting of our sins → We confess with our mouth Jesus as Lord and believe in our heart God raised Him from the dead → God saves us by His grace through faith → We receive the Holy Spirit and become a child of God → We are water baptized → We start basic Gospel training.

BRIAN BENTON

General Order

In the army of God, we have a general order from headquarters found in Romans 13:8, Galatians 5:14, and James 2:8: "Love your neighbor as yourself." To further simplify the general order, Galatians 5:14 says, "For the whole law is fulfilled in one word, in the statement, "You shall love your neighbor as yourself." What is the one word? The one word is LOVE. First John 4:19 says, "We love God because God loved us first". Our response to God loving us first is we love God with everything we are and in everything we do.

In Matthew Chapter 22:34-40, the Pharisees asked Jesus, "What is the great commandment?" Jesus responded that we should love God with all our heart, soul, and mind, and we should love our neighbor as ourselves. So we love God with everything we are in response to His love for us, and His love is what changes us from the inside out. He is the Potter, and we are the clay. He wants to conform us into the image of Jesus, who is the standard of how to love.

Since God first loved us, our response to His love is to love God. Since we love God, we're going to love ourselves because God created us. Since God created us out of love, we will obey what God says and glorify Him in everything we do. Since God loves us, we love ourselves, and we love our neighbor because God created our neighbor and loves our neighbor. Since, we don't want our neighbor to hurt from sin or experience death, we're going to love them as Jesus loved and share the Gospel with them so that they will know Jesus.

The general order is simple: love God, love people, make disciples—and in everything—glorify God.

If we reverse engineer what happened in the Garden of Eden, man failed to love his neighbor. If Adam would have loved God, he would have never rebelled against God. If Adam would have loved his neighbor, Eve, as himself, he would not have let Eve be deceived by Satan. If Eve would have loved her neighbor, Adam, like herself, she would not have eaten the fruit and influenced Adam to eat the fruit. The consequence of sin is broken relationships, but the power of love is restored relationships. The love of God demonstrated through the life, death, and resurrection of Jesus restores our relationship with God forever. The love of God empowers us to obey God and love our neighbor as ourself.

Selfless Service

The command "love your neighbor as yourself" is first recorded in Leviticus 19:18 under the old covenant. In the new covenant, Jesus continues that command but raises the standard of loving our neighbor as ourselves by showing us the standard. In John 15:12, Jesus tells the disciples, "This is My commandment, that you love one another, just as I have loved you." Jesus came to the earth to serve, not to be served and gave His life as a ransom for many (Matthew 20 and Mark 10).

In the new covenant we are instructed to, "Do nothing from selfishness or empty conceit, but with humility of mind regard one another as more important than yourselves; do not merely look out for your own personal interests, but also for the interest of others. Have this attitude in yourselves, which was also in Christ Jesus, who although He existed in the form of God, did not regard equality with God a thing to be grasped, but emptied Himself, taking the form of a bond-servant, and being made in the likeness of men.

Being found in appearance as a man, He humbled himself by becoming obedient to the point of death, even death on a cross" (Philippians 2:3-8).

In the new covenant, we are also instructed to die to ourselves (Matthew 16 and Mark 8) and become a living sacrifice (Romans 12 and Ephesians 5). When we die to ourselves as an act of selfless service, we present our bodies to God as living and holy sacrifices. The love of God grows in us and flows out of us to love our neighbor as Jesus loves our neighbor.

Faith and Trust

Faith and trust sometimes are used as interchangeable words, but they are different. The word faith is a noun, and the word trust is a verb. When I lived in Eugene, Oregon in my late teens, a door-to-door salesman knocked on my door selling cleaning products. I opened the door and listened to his pitch. He showed me a spray bottle with cleaner and explained the benefits of how well his product cleaned and how safe the product was to use. He demonstrated his faith in the product by trusting the product was safe enough to consume by untwisting the top of the spray bottle and licking the plastic tube with the cleaning solution on it. The sales pitch was so convincing that I gained faith in the product and demonstrated my trust in the product by purchasing it.

According to Hebrews 11:1, "Faith is the certainty of things hoped for, a proof of things not seen", and James 2:26 says, "Faith without works is dead." Faith and trust are both fundamental to our relationship with God.

Trust is acting based on our faith in God. We can have faith in God because He cannot lie, and we trust God by doing what He says (Titus 1:2, Numbers 23:19, Hebrews 6:18). We can have faith in what God is doing now and in what He's going to do in the future because He has declared the end from the beginning (Isaiah 46:10). The more faith we have in God the more we trust God and advance His Kingdom with love.

The more we love people, the more we honor people; and the more trust we extend to people, the more trust we gain from people. The more faith and trust we have in our relationship with God and people, the more our relationship will grow with God and people. The less faith and trust we have in our relationships, the less healthy our relationships become with one another.

Jesus completely trusted the Father and obeyed the Father to build the Kingdom of God. Because the disciples placed their faith in Jesus and trusted what He said, Jesus trusted them to advance His Kingdom and commissioned them to "go and make disciples." Jesus is the Author and Perfecter of our faith who helps increase our faith so that we trust in Him more (Hebrews 12:2). Jesus extends His trust to us by giving us more responsibility as we are faithful in the small things (Luke 16:10). The small things in our lives start with loving our neighbor as ourselves, then God increases our responsibility the more we trust and obey.

At times our faith in God may decrease or even fail depending on how we allow circumstances to cause us to doubt. We may fail to trust God because of a lack of faith. In Matthew 14, Jesus left the disciples in a boat while He went onto a mountain to pray alone at night. The wind was very strong causing the waves to batter the boat. Jesus started walking on water at night towards the disciples, and they thought He was a ghost. Jesus made it clear it was Him.

Peter said to Jesus, "Lord, if it is You, command me to come to You on the water." And Jesus said, "Come!" (Matthew 14:28-29) Then Peter walked on water until he saw the wind, became frightened, and started sinking. He cried out to the Lord to save him. Immediately Jesus reached out His hand and took hold of Peter. Peter's faith in Jesus failed because he became focused on his circumstance instead of staying focused on Jesus. When your faith in God begins to fail, remember that the love of God never fails (1 Corinthians 13:8). He is causing all things to work together for good to those who love God (Romans 8:28).

BRIAN BENTON

Communication

When military forces go to battle, they communicate with their chain of command and fellow soldiers. As soldiers of Christ, we cannot battle sin, the world, or the forces of darkness without communicating with our chain of command: God. The military uses call signs as unique identifiers in military communications. As soldiers of Christ, we have a call sign that helps us battle sin, overcome the world, and knock the forces of darkness out of the battle space. Our call sign is to pray to the Father in Jesus' name.

We can pray to the Father in Jesus' name because we are children of God. As children of God, we have a parent-child relationship with the Father. Jesus tells us in Matthew 7:11, "If you then, being evil, know how to give good gifts to your children, how much more will your Father who is in heaven give what is good to those who ask Him!" Not only is the Father a good gift giver, but He already knows what we are going to pray before we pray (Isaiah 46:9-10).

You may be wondering, if that is true then why do we need to pray? We pray as an act of faith and trust that we are completely dependent on God. We pray not to change the will of God, but to be changed by the will of God.

When we pray to the Father in Jesus' name, we have an advocate in heaven who sits on a throne of grace who can sympathize with our weaknesses (Hebrews 4:15). Jesus understands what are going through and cares for us. When we pray to the Father in Jesus' name we are empowered, encouraged, comforted, and helped by the Holy Spirit (John 14:16-17 and Romans 8:26).

When we communicate with our fellow soldiers in Christ and with others, we are to speak life. The Word of God tells us in Proverbs 18:21 that life and death is in the power of the tongue. James 3:8 tells us the tongue is full of deadly poison. Our words have the power to restore relationships or sever relationships. Our words have the power to encourage one another or discourage one another.

Our words have the power to save people or send people to die. Our words have the power to encourage someone's potential or limit someone's potential. A great example of how words can encourage someone's potential with God's help is found in Judges Chapter 6.

In Judges 6, the Israelites did what was evil in the sight of the Lord, and the Lord handed them over to the Midians. The Israelites made strongholds in the mountains and caves to protect themselves from the Midians. When the Israelites had sown crops, the Midians teamed up with the Amalekites to destroy all their crops, which left no sustenance for Israel. Israel was brought very low and cried out to the Lord for help.

The Lord sent an angel to Gideon who was the youngest in his family, and his family was the least among the place where he lived. The angel spoke this to Gideon, "The Lord is with you, valiant warrior" (Judges 6:12). Gideon had no idea that he would become a valiant warrior, but the angel spoke life and potential to Gideon. Gideon doubted himself and God several times, but God encouraged him every step of the way to move towards his potential.

In Judges Chapter 7, Gideon equipped 300 men with trumpets and pitchers with torches in it. They surrounded the camp of Midian at night and then blew their trumpets and smashed their pitchers with their hands. Immediately afterwards they shouted, "A sword for the Lord and for Gideon" (Judges 7:20). Then the Lord turned the sword against one another in the Midian camp, and the entire army fled.

Battle Cry

In ancient warfare, military units used battle cries to motivate their troops to advance and scare their opponents. In spiritual warfare, our battle cry against the forces of darkness is our praise to God. When we praise God, we trust who God is, what He has done, and what He is going to do. Our praise to God strengthens our trust in Him and builds up our faith to act according to His will. Our praise to God strengthens the faith of others around us to trust God more and builds up their faith.

Praising God continually and giving thanks to His Name is an act of sacrifice (Hebrews 13:15) that takes the focus off ourselves, our circumstances, and the world. Praising God allows us to focus on who God is, thank Him for what He has done, and thank Him for what He is going to do according to His will. Praising God is more than what we do in our mind. It is giving thanks to His Name with our lips (Hebrews 13:15) and speaking psalms, hymns, and songs from the Spirit (Ephesians 5:19).

Praising God softens our hearts and minds to receive what He wants to teach us and what He wants to do in us and through us. There have been many times in my life when the Holy Spirit has revealed His will to me as I was praising Him.

In April of 2015, I was in my "prayer garage" praising God and praying to Him for about an hour. I had struggled with loneliness as a single man, but I trusted in God that He would provide me with a wife. At the end of that hour, God gave me a vision that I would have three children, so I knew I would get married and have a family one day.

In April of 2016, during a Wednesday night worship gathering, I was praising God alongside my girlfriend at the time, Christy, and I felt prompted to ask Father God for permission to marry her. He told me to "Go", so I obeyed. We got married on May 29, 2016. I immediately became a stepfather to Mark Wesley, who became my first child. Christy and I obeyed the Bible to be fruitful and multiply, and she became pregnant with Maverick Wyatt, my second child.

In the Summer of 2017, during a Sunday morning worship service, I was praising God alongside Christy who was pregnant with our third child, but we didn't know the gender. While I was singing praises, the Holy Spirit revealed to me that Christy was having a girl. Later that summer, Christy joined a women's bible study group with the Pregnancy Resource Center in Benton. After a few weeks attending the group, they asked her if she would be an ultrasound model for their annual fundraising gala.

Christy accepted their invitation and became the model. As I watched my baby girl, Malone Whitely, displayed on a video screen in front of 600 people at the gala, I was reminded of God's faithfulness and the vision He gave me in April 2015 that I would have three children.

It might not be easy to praise God in the bad times or when we don't get what we want, but training ourselves to praise God always increases our faith in who God is, what He has done, and what He is going to do according to His will. Praising God is our battle cry declaring Jesus has won the victory, regardless of our circumstances.

Rest

We will never be as effective as we can be advancing the Kingdom of God without spiritual, physical, and emotional rest. As children of God, we can rest spiritually in our identity because of what Jesus has done for us and where we are going... heaven. Before Jesus did one work of ministry, the Father declared, "This is my beloved Son, with whom I am well pleased" (Matthew 3:17). When we place our faith in Jesus as Lord and believe in our heart God raised Him from the dead, we are saved and become children of God.

As children of God, the Father is well pleased in us because we are His children. We can rest in our identity that we don't have to do good works to maintain our identity. A "works" based theology can lead you to believe your identity is based on doing "good works" to please God, which can also lead to an unhealthy fear that you might go to hell for not doing enough "good works" or for falling back into sin. We work out our salvation with fear and trembling, allowing God to work through us for His good pleasure (Philippians 2:12-13).

It's a type of "fear and trembling" knowing that if it wasn't for the salvation provided by Jesus, we would live a life of fear and worry. In the presence of God there is no fear or worry. As children of God we are always in the presence of God because the Holy Spirit lives inside of us. We can rest in our identity as children of God, not because of what we have done or didn't do, but because of what Jesus has done and who He is.

As humans, we need spiritual, physical, and emotional rest because they are all interconnected. God created the heavens and the earth in six days and rested on the seventh day. God didn't need to rest on the seventh day, but He rested for man's benefit. The fourth commandment of the ten commandments recorded in Exodus 20:8-10 says, "Remember the Sabbath day, to keep it holy. Six days you shall labor and do all your work, but the seventh day is a Sabbath of the Lord your God..." Under the new covenant we are not bound to the Law because we are under Grace. However, the principle of resting from work at least one day per week is very beneficial for us spiritually, emotionally, and physically.

Our sleep can be impacted by our physical, emotional, and spiritual health. If we are anxious, angry, depressed, stressed, or sick when we go to bed, we may not be able to rest well, which will negatively impact us the following day or days. If we are not resting well, we need to identify the cause and act so that we can rest well. Sleep is very important for our overall rest.

As humans, we are going to experience different emotions at different times in our lives, but it's not good to be sad all the time, depressed all the time, angry all the time, frustrated all the time, stressed all the time, or worried all the time. We need to let our emotions rest! If you watch something or listen to something that makes you sad all the time, I advise you to stop watching it or listening to it—to rest from the sadness. If you get angry or frustrated all the time, I recommend re-evaluating your expectations of people, places, and things—to rest from anger and frustration. We live in an imperfect world with imperfect people, places, and things. We will be let down by people, places, and things throughout our entire life. Jesus told the disciples, "In this world you have tribulations" (John 16:33).

Stress in our lives is generally caused by a lack of margin, whether it be time margin, relational margin, or financial margin. The more we try to do in a day in an imperfect world with imperfect people, places, and things, the more our expectations are not met. This can cause stress. I recommend doing less, delegating more, and eliminating everything that doesn't glorify God—to rest from time-based stress.

The less kindness, compassion, grace, patience, and forgiveness we demonstrate in our relationships, the more stress can be caused in those relationships. I recommend resting from relational stress with more kindness, compassion, grace, patience, and forgiveness.

The same is true for our finances. The less margin we have in our bank account and the more margin we have in debt, the more financial stress we'll have. I recommend resting from financial stress by creating a simple budget, giving to the Kingdom, spending less than you make, paying off your debt, and making wise investments.

In addition to spiritual, physical, and emotional rest, I recommend you create moments of rest from technology. In this modern age, we are distracted more than ever with access to anything, anytime, and anywhere. I don't think God designed us to take in an infinite amount of information with a finite mind. Only God can process an infinite amount of information, because He is infinite. The internet, technology, and media can be a blessing and a curse. There is so much information and content available that we can get easily distracted and waste minutes, hours, days, months, and years watching or listening to stuff that doesn't help us advance God's Kingdom with love.

Dress Code

The military uses a dress code to differentiate their branches of service, units, and ranks by what they wear. Well, we have a dress code too in the Kingdom of God to differentiate ourselves from the world. We are called to be different—to be salt and light in this dark world (Matthew 5:13-14). We are also called to not be conformed to the patterns of this world (Romans 12:2).

Romans 13:12 tells us to "put on the armor of light", and Ephesians 6:11-12 expounds on Romans 13:12 by adding, "put on the full armor of God, so that we will be able to stand firm against the schemes of the devil." We are in a spiritual war against the worldly forces of darkness and against the spiritual forces of wickedness in the heavenly places.

We can't fight in this war without the Lord Jesus Christ and His armor. We put on the belt of truth so that all the other armor is held together. We put on the breastplate of righteousness to guard our hearts. We strap on our feet the preparation of the Gospel of peace because we are commissioned to advance the Gospel. We take up the shield of faith to extinguish all flaming arrows from the enemy. We take the helmet of salvation to guard our minds and the sword of the Spirit to fight the good fight of faith. The sword of the Spirit is the Word of God (Ephesians 6:10-17).

Colossians 3:12-14 tells us to put on a heart of compassion, kindness, humility, gentleness, and patience—bearing with one another and forgiving one another just as the Lord forgave you. In addition to all those things, we put on love, which is the perfect bond of unity.

Diet

Every military unit needs a healthy supply of food to sustain the military unit and help it advance. When the food supply is unhealthy the military unit can become unhealthy and unable to advance. In the Kingdom of God, aka "The Lords Army", our diet is to live on every word that comes out of the mouth of God (Matthew 4:4). We are not to eat "cotton candy sin." I first heard the term "cotton candy sin" from Ryan Ries, and it has stuck ever since.

In Matthew 5:6, the Word of God tells us to hunger and thirst for righteousness, and we will be satisfied. Our flesh craves the cotton candy sin of the world, but it never satisfies our hunger or thirst. Galatians 5:19-21 gives us a list of what the cotton candy sins, the deeds of the flesh, are: sexual immorality, impurity, indecent behavior, idolatry, witchcraft, hostilities, strife, jealously, outbursts of anger, selfish ambition, dissensions, factions, envy, drunkenness, carousing, and things like these.

Jesus is the bread of life, living water, and righteousness. When we hunger for the bread of life and thirst for the living water, we draw near to Jesus who is righteousness, and we are filled with the fruit of the Spirit: Love, Joy, Peace, Patience, Kindness, Goodness, Faithfulness, Gentleness, and Self Control (Galatians 5:22-23). There is no law on how much Love, Joy, Peace, Patience, Kindness, Goodness, Faithfulness, Gentleness, and Self Control we are filled with. When we stay close to Jesus we can taste and see He is good (Psalm 34:8). We don't have to worry about the painful and negative side effects of cotton candy sin.

In 1 Timothy 4:6, Paul wrote to Timothy encouraging him to constantly nourish himself with the words of the faith and of the sound doctrine he had been following. We, too, need to heed the words Paul wrote to Timothy to constantly nourish ourselves by reading the Word of God and following sound doctrine so that we don't fall away from the faith by paying attention to deceitful spirits and teachings of demons (1 Timothy 4:1). Satan wants us to feed on cotton candy false doctrine that looks good, smells goods, and even tastes good so that we advance his dark kingdom rather than advancing God's Kingdom with love.

In terms of our physical needs, we should eat and drink in a way that glorifies God and fuels our body to operate as the temple of the Holy Spirit. Living and walking by the Spirit of God increases our self control to avoid unhealthy food and drink as well as overindulging. Loving our neighbor as ourselves helps us to love our bodies because God created our body and loves us.

Exercise

In military basic training, a drill sergeant helps discipline recruits through pull-ups, push-ups, running, obstacle courses, and other exercises to increase their mental and physical toughness. In terms of physical exercise, we do need to exercise our bodies so that it is healthy and able to advance the Kingdom of God with love. However, the investment of disciplining our mind and body through physical exercise is only slightly beneficial since the results are finite. Paul taught Timothy to discipline himself for the purpose of godliness and explains that godliness is beneficial in all things and holds promise for the present life and for the life to come (1 Timothy 4:7).

We also need to discipline ourselves for the purpose of godliness. When we exercise godliness, we build up our faith-muscles to trust God more and advance His Kingdom with love. I've included five core exercises to build your faith-muscles and encourage others:

Exercise 1: Learn the Word of God and do what it says

In 2 Timothy 3:16-17 we are instructed to be fully capable, equipped for every good work by learning the Word of God. James 1:22-23 instructs us to prove we know the Word of God by doing what it says.

Exercise 2: Rejoice, pray, and think godly thoughts

In Philippians 4:4-9, we are instructed to rejoice in the Lord always, pray for everything with thanksgiving, and think about things that are honorable, right, pure, lovely, commendable, excellent, and praiseworthy.

Exercise 3: Give thanks in everything

In 1 Thessalonians 5:18, we are instructed to give thanks in everything because it is the will of God. Does that mean we are to give thanks in all our trials, tribulations, pain, sicknesses, sorrow, loss, lack as well as our times of joy, abundance, peace, health, etc.?

Yes, we are to give thanks in everything! Why should we give thanks in everything? When we give thanks in all circumstances we are trusting in God, acting on faith that He is good, and declaring He is good!

When people around us hear us give thanks to God regardless of our circumstances, we help point them to God so they can learn that God is good. As it says in Psalm 107:1-2, "Give thanks to the Lord, for He is good, for His mercy is everlasting. The redeemed of the Lord shall say so, those whom He has redeemed from the hand of the enemy." Not only can we give thanks because He is good, but He causes all things to work together for good (Romans 8:28). When you are going through a trial, tribulation, pain, sickness, sorrow, loss, or anything else, remember God is going to cause good to come out of it. Thank you, Lord, for You are good!

Exercise 4: Fellowship

In Acts 2:42 we are provided with a model to continually learn, fellowship, break bread, and pray with other believers. In Hebrews 10:25, we are told not to give up meeting together so that we may encourage one another.

Exercise 5: Speak life

In Ephesians 4:15 we are instructed to speak truth in love, and Ephesians 4:29 tells us to speak only what is good, helpful, and encouraging to those that listen. Foul language, crude jokes, abusive speech, and anything else unwholesome is unacceptable to come out of our mouths.

Unit Building

The first unit in the Kingdom of God is God! God is revealed in Scripture as three persons known as the Trinity: Father, Son, and Holy Spirit.

Father God is our Good Shepherd (John 10:11-18), Provider (Matthew 6:32-33), and Disciplinarian (Hebrews 12:4-11).

The Son of God is Lord and Savior (Luke 2:11), King of kings (1 Timothy 6:15), Shepherd (John 10:11-18), Judge (John 5:22), Advocate (Hebrews 4:12), High Priest (Hebrews 4:14-16), and Friend (John 15:14-15).

The Holy Spirit is our Strength and Prayer Intercessor (Romans 8:26). He is our Helper, Teacher, Counselor, Advocate, and Guide (John 14:16-31).

The second unit in the Kingdom of God is the angelic army, and the third unit is the family of God, aka the Church.

God's plan in Genesis was for Adam and Eve to multiply and create a family. Adam and Eve would teach their children to worship God, and they would grow up, marry, multiply, and teach their children to worship God. God wanted a big family of human beings that multiplied through the institution of marriage and the family.

However, it didn't take man long to become so wicked that God flooded the earth. In Genesis Chapter 6, God chose to save a man named Noah and his family from the flood by teaching them how to build a large boat called an "Ark" large enough to carry his family and every male and female animal pair.

Noah trusted God and acted on his faith in God to build the Ark. God made a covenant with Noah and with his descendants that He would never again destroy the earth by a flood in Genesis Chapter 9.

God raised up the nation of Israel as His chosen people after the flood. The Israelites would obey God for a season, then disobey God for a season. God would bring judgement against the Israelites, then the Israelites would repent and obey God again. The cycle reoccurred throughout the Old Testament with the nation of Israel rising and falling.

God's plan to build His Kingdom on the earth appeared not to be working, however the plan was actually working just as God had intended. God allowed "man" to be the problem in His plan so that the solution in His plan would be the "Son of Man." God chose the nation of Israel to bring forth the Gospel to all nations through the "Son of Man" Jesus Christ. When people repent and believe the Gospel, two important things happen related to the institution of marriage and the family.

First, we become a part of the bride of Christ and are married to Jesus Christ. Earthly marriages can end in divorce, but the marriage to Christ is an everlasting covenant that is unbreakable and cannot end in divorce (Ephesians 5:25-32).

Second, we become born again children of God (John 1:12). Children of earthly families can be disowned, abused, forgotten, or given up for adoption, but in the family of God no one can snatch us out of the Father's hand (John 10:29)!

God's Kingdom building strategy hasn't changed since the Garden of Eden. Kingdom building starts in the home with the family. The New Testament church operated in the temple and private homes with brothers and sisters in Christ "devoting themselves to the apostles' teaching and to fellowship, to the breaking of bread and to prayer" (Acts 2:42). The believers would obey what they were taught, which was to make disciples in their home and then go outside the walls of their home to make disciples. Kingdom building starts in the home within the family, then multiplies outside the home.

Jesus invested three years of His life with His "small group" of the twelve disciples. He taught them, fellowshipped with them, broke bread with them, and prayed with them. He sent them out in pairs of two (Mark 6:7) because two are stronger than one (Ecclesiastes 4:9-12).

When each disciple made a disciple, the Kingdom of God doubled. When each of the four disciples made a disciple, then the Kingdom of God doubled again, and there were eight disciples. When each of the eight disciples made a disciple, then the Kingdom of God doubled again, and there were sixteen disciples. As you can see, the multiplication of the Kingdom of God grows exponentially as the Spirit of God saves people and as disciples continue to make disciples.

Navigation Training

In military basic training, soldiers can be trained how to navigate land, sea, and air. In Gospel basic training, our navigation training is to read the Word of God and trust Jesus who is the Word of God. The Word of God is a lamp unto our feet and a light unto our path (Psalm 119:105). We walk by faith and not by sight because we trust Jesus (2 Corinthians 5:7).

We have "light vision" instead of night vision because we obey what Jesus said, to not let our eyes become unhealthy, which fills our whole bodies with darkness (Matthew 6:22-23).

We have "Kingdom vision" instead of worldly vision because we obey what Jesus said to seek first His Kingdom and His righteousness (Matthew 6:33). We help people in darkness find the light by loving them like Jesus and sharing the Gospel with them.

Reconnaissance Training

In ancient times, the role of the watchman was critical to protect cities and military installations. A watchman was typically stationed on a city wall, a watch tower, or in a forward position. They were trained to look out for and report on potential danger or surprise enemy attacks. In modern military, the role of the watchman has advanced into what is known as reconnaissance. In reconnaissance training, soldiers are trained to look out for and report on the position, activities, resources, strengths, and weaknesses of potential enemies.

In Gospel basic training, the first enemy to look out for is ourselves. We must watch out for our pride, watch out for what we allow to enter our minds, watch out for what we allow to enter our bodies, watch out for who we hang around with, watch out where we hang out at, and watch out for anything we allow to become an idol in our lives.

The Apostle Paul explains the consequences of Israel's sin in 1 Corinthians 10:1-11. It is used as an example for us to not crave evil things. Even though we may not think we could fall into the same sins of Israel or the same sins of other people, temptation is inside all of us, and we can fall at any time. That's why Paul warns us in 1 Corinthians 10:12, "Therefore let the one who thinks he stands watch out that he does not fall." Then Paul encourages us in 1 Corinthians 10:13 how to overcome temptation, "No temptation has overtaken you except something common to mankind; and God is faithful, so He will not allow you to be tempted beyond what you are able, but with the temptation will provide the way of escape also, so that you will be able to endure it."

We can rest in the fact that God knows we will be tempted, and God will provide the way of escape from temptation. Our responsibility is to look for the way of escape, and escape!

The second enemy to look out for is isolation. When we are isolated, we don't have anyone looking out for us and checking on us. We can fall prey to the schemes of the devil who "prowls around like a roaring lion, seeking someone to devour" (1 Peter 5:8).

In the animal kingdom, the lion is at the top of the food chain on land. If a lion is hungry for lamb chops, the lion, by instinct, will look for the sheep that is isolated from the flock to attack and kill. The role of the shepherd is to watch out for, protect, and guide the sheep to stay within the flock. The same is true for us. We must stay connected to the flock under the protection of the shepherd. We stay connected to the flock through the local church by attending regular worship gatherings and small group gatherings. We stay under the protection of the shepherd by obeying the leaders of the local church because they keep watch over our souls and will give an account according to Hebrews 13:17.

The third enemy to look out for is selfishness. We can't love our neighbor as ourselves if we are selfish. We need our neighbors to look out for us and check on us, just as they need us to look out for them and check on them. We love one another by looking out for one another.

Battle Training

Military Units train how they are going to communicate, navigate terrain, dismount vehicles, deal with chemical/biological attacks, evacuate the wounded, and fight the enemy so that when they are in battle they can react quickly and know what to do. Similarly, in the army of God, we also need to train for combat. We don't wrestle against flesh and blood in the physical realm, but we fight against dark forces in the spiritual realm (Ephesians 6:12).

The dark forces disguise their attacks with cotton candy sin, twisted truth, and "good things" that distract us from godly things. Sometimes they attack us in stealth mode so that we don't know we are under attack. Other times they roar like a lion or appear as big as a giant to scare us. God allows the dark forces to attack us so that we will stay close to Him, stay close to other believers, and put on His armor to fight the forces of darkness.

When David fought the Philistine giant named Goliath, he didn't have any formal military combat training. He refused to wear the armor provided by King Saul. Goliath was big, strong, well armored, and well trained in hand-to-hand combat. As a shepherd, David had fought off and killed both lions and bears to protect his flock (1 Samuel 17).

David had faith in God to protect him and had trusted God when he killed the lion and the bear. From David's point of view, fighting and killing Goliath was no different from his experience with the lion and the bear. David had faith in God to rescue him and trusted God when he killed Goliath in the presence of the entire Philistine army. David didn't know that one day he would face and kill a giant, but he was prepared because he had faith in God. We too can be prepared for battle by having faith in God. The best way to demonstrate our faith is to trust God by submitting to His will daily. The more we trust God, the more our faith in God grows.

When an army wins a battle and offers peace terms to their opponent, the opponent has the option to continue fighting or accept the peace terms. In our lives we can continue to battle against God's will or accept the peace that comes from obeying His will. In our lives we can battle against asking others for forgiveness when we've wronged someone, or we can make peace by asking for forgiveness.

In our lives we can battle against forgiving others for a wrong they've committed against us, or we can make peace with them by forgiving them. When we fall into sin we can battle against asking God for forgiveness and confessing our sins to others, or we can ask God to forgive us and confess our sins to others, so we can be healed. The more we train in asking for forgiveness, offering forgiveness, and confessing our sins, the more peace we will have in our relationship with God and with people.

We all battle temptation in our lives, but we can't battle it in our own strength. We are most vulnerable to temptation when we are fatigued, isolated, and when we think we are no longer susceptible to temptation. According to 1 John 2:16, there are three ways we are tempted: the lust of the flesh, the lust of the eyes, and the pride of life.

Overcoming temptation is a work of the Spirit of God and because of the grace of God. The Word of God gives us practical advice on how to train ourselves to battle temptation: Escape from it! Don't try to battle the temptation but look for the way of escape and flee from it. First Corinthians 10:13 promises us a way of escape so that we will be able to endure the temptation. We must train ourselves to look for the way of escape and flee from the temptation.

If there's a situation or a place that could potentially cause us to be tempted, then we should escape from that temptation by not going there. If we find ourselves in a situation or in a place where we are being tempted, then we should escape by going somewhere else. If we find ourselves in a place of isolation where we could become tempted, we should escape from being in insolation by surrounding ourselves with other believers.

If we could be tempted by electronics, then escape from the temptation by using accountability software, creating distance between yourself and the electronics, or placing the electronics in an area other people can see. Don't let your guard down when it comes to temptation or look at others struggling with a temptation and think you will never give into that temptation. First Corinthians 10:12 tells us, "Therefore let the one who thinks he stands watch out that he does not fall." We must stay humble, stay guarded, stay close to Jesus, and stay away from people, places, and things that can cause us to be tempted.

When we go to battle, we can't go without armor, weapons, ground forces, and air support. In the army of God, we submit completely to King Jesus and obey His commands. We wear the full armor of God in battle and take up our offensive weapon, the sword of the Spirit, to battle against the lies and deception of the enemy.

We join forces with our brothers and sisters in Christ across the world to battle the enemy and to love one another as Jesus loves. We call in heavenly air strikes through prayer to help us advance God's Kingdom with love. If all the above is too much to remember, just ask Jesus to fight for you and through you!

Rules of Engagement

Military units are given a set of rules on how to engage the enemy, known as rules of engagement. In the army of God our rule for engaging people in this world is to love one another like Jesus. Loving one another is serving one another, praying for one another, being in the trenches with one another when life gets tough, grieving with one another during a loss or setback, listening to one another, being patient with one another, being kind to one another, sharing with one another, rejoicing with one another, having fun with one another, encouraging one another, and speaking life to one another.

Loving one another is trying to find common ground with everyone. Loving one another is building relationships based on common courtesy and respect. Loving one another is becoming someone's friend without expecting anything from them. Loving one another like Jesus is our rule for engaging with people in the world.

Supply Chain

The supply chain in military operations is a matter of life and death for an army. If an army is not well supplied with food, water, ammunition, fuel, etc., they can become vulnerable to defeat. Napoleon Bonaparte built a grand army of over 500,000 men to invade Russia in 1812. Napoleon wanted to advance quickly and rely on plundering supplies in Russian territory instead of waiting to be supplied. The Russian military command played a game of cat and mouse, drawing Napoleon and his grand army further and further into Russian Territory while burning any supplies Napoleon's army could plunder. Napoleon's army wasn't equipped to deal with the Russian winter and ran out of supplies. In short, Napoleon was defeated by a poor supply chain for his army.

In the army of God, we have a supply chain that is underfunded and undersupplied by man. According to Nonprofit Source, in 2018 only ten to twenty-five percent of people gave ten percent of their income regularly. Giving to the local church and ministries funds the supply chain to advance God's Kingdom with love. To love our neighbor as ourself requires our time, energy, resources, and money.

God doesn't need our money, resources, or anything else. He already owns everything and can speak what He wants into existence with His word. God allows us to partner with Him to build His Kingdom. He multiplies what we invest into His Kingdom to advance His Kingdom.

The supply chain in the army of God helps fund the operations of the local church and missions outreach. It helps care for the spiritually wounded, provide homes for orphans, care for widows, and meals for the hungry. It gives shelter for the homeless, medical care for the sick, counseling for the hurting, recovery for the addict, sight for the blind, money for the poor, opportunities for the weak, comfort for the hurting, and help for special needs—just to name a few.

When the COVID-19 lockdowns and shutdowns started in March 2020, I felt led to double my giving and did so with great joy, even though there was economic uncertainty. At the end of 2020, my business grew fifty-six percent compared to 2019. I credit God's faithfulness and goodness.

War Story

There are many war stories passed down through the ages of epic battles—amazing acts of valor and famous generals—but there is only one story that matters for eternity: The story of Jesus. The story of Jesus is the greatest victory in the history of the universe. He defeated sin, Satan, the world, and death.

We can share about His victory through our personal testimony. Our personal testimony is how we overcame by the blood of the Lamb (Revelation 12:11). No one will know about our personal testimony unless we share it with others.

To share your testimony with others, I recommend writing it down by asking four questions:

1. How was your life before knowing Jesus?
2. How did you come to know Jesus?
3. How is your life now after knowing Jesus?
4. What are you doing now to advance His Kingdom?

After you write down your testimony, I recommend you memorize it and practice sharing it so you will be ready. As you continue your faith journey, you can review your testimony from time to time as a reminder of God's faithfulness.

Memorial Service

A military funeral is performed for all military personnel killed in action with various military elements such as honor guard, the firing of volley shots, drumming, and draping a flag over the coffin. In the army of God, we remember the sacrifice Jesus made being killed in action to save us from our sin. We refer to this as the Lord's Supper, or communion.

The elements for communion are bread and a drink from the fruit of the vine. The drink can be wine or grape juice. The bread represents the body of Christ and the drink of the fruit of the vine represents the blood of the new covenant. When we take communion, we are to take it in a worthy manner and examine ourselves as we remember the sacrifice of Jesus (Matthew 26:26-29, Mark 14:22-25, Luke 22:19-20, 1 Corinthians 11:17-33).

Graduation

At the end of military basic training, there is a graduation ceremony honoring everyone who has completed the training. In Gospel basic training there is no graduation ceremony, but there is lifelong training in loving God, loving people, making disciples, and glorifying God in everything we do. At the end of our life on Earth, we will be "promoted to glory", a term used by the Salvation Army to describe the death of a Salvationist.

Gospel Occupational Specialty

After completing military basic training, you start training in your Military Occupational Specialty (MOS) to learn the skills to perform the duties of your respective specialty. Every occupational specialty serves an important function in the operation of the military. If everyone did the same function, the military would be very limited.

In the Kingdom of God, we all have a Gospel Occupational Specialty (GOS), or as described in the Bible, "a calling" and "part of the body of Christ." Every calling and part of the body of Christ works together to advance the Kingdom of God with love.

Our specific calling might be seasonal, or it might be for a lifetime. It just depends on the assignment by the Holy Spirit. We may serve in children's ministry for a season, in high school ministry for a season, or in one of those ministries for a lifetime. Regardless of our calling, we must be careful we don't fall into the trap of comparison with others.

We live in a globally connected world where we have the opportunity to compare ourselves at anytime to anyone. We can compare our bodies, personal lives, children, possessions, businesses, churches, cars, and anything else. We can compare our callings with other people's callings, our assignments with other people's assignments, and our gifts with other people's gifts. We can compare our relational positions with the relational positions of others. Even Jesus' closest disciples compared themselves to one another.

In John Chapter 21, Jesus appeared to the disciples at the sea of Tiberias after His resurrection. At first they didn't recognize Him (even though this was His third appearance to the disciples), but John—the disciple whom Jesus loved—recognized it was the Lord and told Peter.

Peter threw himself in the sea while the disciples came in a little boat dragging a net full of fish. Jesus had breakfast ready for the disciples and asked them to bring some of the fish they had caught. Peter hauled the net full of large fish which totaled 153. Jesus invited the disciples to have breakfast. When they had finished eating, Jesus asked Peter three times if he loved Him and in doing so reaffirmed Peter three times to fulfill his calling. At the end of Peter's affirmation, Jesus told Peter how He would die and glorify God. Then He tells Peter to "Follow Me!" (John 21:19)

While Jesus was walking with Peter, John must have been following behind them because Peter turned around and saw John. Upon seeing John, Peter said to Jesus, "Lord, and what about this man?" Jesus said to him, "If I want him to remain until I come, what is that to you? You follow me!" (vs. 21-22) Peter was comparing his calling and faith journey to John's instead of focusing on following Jesus and fulfilling his unique calling.

Peter was the first disciple to recognize Jesus as the Christ, the son of the living God. Peter was the first disciple to get out of a boat in a storm to walk on water when he saw Jesus. As long as Peter fixed his eyes on Jesus, he continued to walk on water. When he turned away from looking at Jesus, he got fearful because he saw the storm, and he fell into the water.

When we compare ourselves to others, we move sideways with our own vision instead of moving forward with Kingdom vision. When we look at our circumstances or someone else's circumstances we move sideways with our own vision instead of moving forward with Kingdom vision. Jesus said in Matthew 6:33, "Seek first His Kingdom and His righteousness." We seek first His Kingdom by aligning our lives with His will. We seek His righteousness by staying close to Jesus and doing what He says.

Hebrews 12:2 tells us to "keep our eyes fixed on Jesus", and Paul writes in 1 Corinthians 9:26-27 to "run in such a way, as not without aim" and to "box in such a way, as not beating the air."

We must fix our eyes on Jesus so we're not running the wrong way or running somebody else's race or wasting time beating the air with no aim. The enemy wants us in a state of comparison to distract us from fulfilling our calling in the Kingdom of God. Comparison not only distracts us from our calling but can also lead us down a path of self-righteousness where we compare our righteousness with other believers' righteousness or lack thereof.

In the story of The Prodigal Son in Luke 15, there are two sons and one father. The younger son requests his share of his father's estate and then leaves home and squanders his estate with wild living. The younger son eventually comes to his senses, humbles himself, admits his sin, and moves towards the father as an act of repentance. When the father hears and sees his younger son, he feels compassion for him and runs and embraces him. He puts his best robe on him, a ring on his finger, and sandals on his feet. He slaughters a calf and throws a big party with music and dancing to celebrate.

The older son becomes angry when he approaches his father's house from the field and discovers the celebration is for his younger brother returning home. His father comes out to plead with him, but the older son is self-righteous, comparing his obedience and stewardship to the disobedience and lack of stewardship of his younger brother.

The older son believed he deserved a celebration for his obedience and stewardship rather than his younger brother.

He compared what his younger brother received to what he thought he should have received. If the older son loved his younger brother as himself, he would have embraced him and joined in the celebration. When we compare our obedience and stewardship with others, we can become self-righteous, focusing on ourselves rather focusing on Jesus and fulfilling what He has called us to do.

In Ephesians 4:1-3, God encourages us to walk in a manner worthy of our calling because our calling is worthy. Whatever that calling is, it's a worthy calling because we've been called by God and are given grace according to the measure of Christ's gift.

Grace is a gift. That means it's something that we don't deserve. We don't deserve it because of our work or because of our qualifications. God is the One who calls and assigns people to specific roles in the body of Christ so that we are all unified and equipped for service. God causes the growth throughout His body so it will be built up in love.

So you may be wondering, what is my calling? We are called to love God, love people, make disciples, and glorify God in everything we do. We have specific callings in the body of Christ. The best way to find your specific calling is to follow Jesus! Peter was a fisherman unequipped for ministry, but Jesus chose him and called him. Peter responded by following Jesus, and he walked in his calling as a fisher of people and later as a shepherd of people. The saying "God doesn't call the equipped, but equips the called" applies to us just like it did for Peter and every other disciple.

Saul, a zealot for the Law and a Pharisee of Pharisees, thought his calling was to persecute the Church. Saul persecuted Christians for a season of his life until he had an encounter with Jesus on the road to Damascus. Saul was chosen and called to bring the Gospel to the Gentiles and suffer for the name of Jesus. Saul responded to the call by following Jesus. His name was changed to Paul and he was transformed from a zealot for the Law to a zealot for the grace of God. Paul suffered for the name of Jesus, preached the Gospel to the Gentiles, wrote over half of the New Testament, planted churches, and raised up overseers.

According to the world, our calling is where our passions meet our strengths. According to the Word of God, "God chose the weak things of the world to shame the strong and the foolish things of the world to shame the wise" (1 Corinthians 1:27).

God may call you to an area you think you are weak or untalented in so He can demonstrate His grace and strength.

God may call you to something you are very talented and strong in to demonstrate that you are not as talented or as strong as you thought without His grace and strength.

God may call you to an area where you had no idea of the hidden talent and gift you possessed until you took a step of obedience to walk in the calling.

God may call you to move to a different city, state, or country where you don't know anyone and are completely dependent on Him.

God may call you to start a business with no experience running a business.

God may call you to start a new career with no experience in that career.

God may call you to start a ministry with no experience running a ministry.

Regardless of where God calls you, He will "equip you in every good thing to do His will, working in us that which is pleasing to His sight, through Jesus Christ, to whom be the glory forever and ever. Amen." (Hebrews 13:21)

Jesus has a specific calling for all of us as members of the body of Christ. Our response is to follow Jesus to discover our calling.

GOSPEL OFFENSE: CHAPTER 6

Air Supremacy

The 20th century experienced some of the biggest wars and development of the most powerful vehicles and aircraft in the history of man. The nuclear aircraft carrier is the most powerful vehicle on the water, while the nuclear submarine is the most powerful vehicle under the water. The M270 is the most powerful vehicle on land, and the B-52 nuke bomber is the most powerful aircraft in the air. Out of all the vehicles and aircraft, the military that controls the air space normally controls the outcome of a war. The same is true when it comes to spiritual warfare.

The enemy of God and man, Satan, is referred to as "the prince of the power of the air" in Ephesians 2:2. The air, as explained by Pastor John MacArthur, is the heavenly space around the earth where Satan rules over the movement of demons.

Satan and his demons want to influence mankind to rebel against God, Ruler over the universe. They specifically want division, strife, hate, and unresolved conflict in the Church to keep us from advancing God's Kingdom with love.

In eternity past, Satan caused a division in heaven, influencing a third of the angels to follow him and rebel against God. We don't know exactly how that went down because the Bible doesn't tell us, but if Satan can influence a third of the angels to rebel in heaven in the presence of God, he can cause rebellion and division in the Church if we give into his influence. Satan appears to have the superior advantage over man, controlling the heavenly air space around the earth.

However, Jesus is infinitely ahead of Satan, and He already knew what Satan had planned to do to the Church. In John 17:20-21, Jesus prayed that we would be one, just as He and the Father are One. God's will for His Church on the earth is to be one unified Church, regardless of our denomination, political affiliation, geographical location, race, and gender.

For us to become one with the Father and Son we must die to what we want to do and allow the Holy Spirit to lead us to do what He wants us to do. For us to be Spirit led, we must discipline ourselves to pray without ceasing, which means to pray all the time. When we pray all the time, we become less dependent on what we want to do and more dependent on what God wants us to do. We become more aware of the presence of the Father, Son, and Holy Spirit in our lives.

In Matthew 6:5-14, Jesus teaches us how to pray. First, He tells us not to pray to be seen by others like the hypocrites do but to go into our inner room, close the door, and pray to the Father in secret. The Father sees what we do in secret and will reward us. The enemy wants us to commit sin in secret to destroy us, but our heavenly Father wants us to pray to Him in secret so that He can reward us.

Second, Jesus tells us that we don't have to pray for the same things repeatedly with many words because our Father knows what we need before we ask Him.

Third, Jesus prays The Lord's Prayer to give us a model to follow when we pray.

In the first verse of The Lord's Prayer, Jesus prays to the Father and acknowledges the Father is in heaven. When we pray to the Father, we should have great reverence for who He is and His name. The only reason we can pray to the Father is because of the finished work of Jesus Christ. He reconciled us to the Father, enabling us to pray to the Father as children of God.

The second verse acknowledges the Father is over the Kingdom and His will be done on earth as it is in heaven. The Father has decreed that His will in heaven will be accomplished in heaven and on the earth regardless of the schemes of Satan or man. This ties in with what Jesus tells us: To "seek first His Kingdom and His righteousness" (Matthew 6:33). We were created by God on purpose for His purpose and His glory. Life is not about what we want to do but rather what He wants us to do. He is Father, and He knows what's best for His children.

The third verse, "Give us this day our daily bread" (Matthew 6:11) may come across like a child demanding their parent give them something. In this context, it is a child of God trusting in the provision of their Father and obeying the Word of God. We need the Word of God to live, just like we need food, drink, shelter, and clothes to live.

The Spirit of God led Jesus to face Satan in the wilderness after forty days and forty nights of fasting. Satan knew that Jesus was physically hungry and tempted Him saying, "If You are the Son of God, command that these stones become bread" (Matthew 4:3).

If Jesus would have given into His hunger and obeyed Satan's command, He would have sinned and failed. However, He rebuked Satan saying that "man shall not live on bread alone, but on every word that comes from the mouth of God" (Matthew 4:4).

After being set free from 400 years of Egyptian slavery, the Spirit of God led the Israelites into the wilderness for forty years for their disobedience of idolatry. The Israelites complained to Moses and Aaron that they were going to die of hunger in the wilderness. The Lord told Moses He would rain bread from heaven, and the Israelites should gather a day's portion every day so that He may test them whether they would walk in His instruction. On the sixth day, the Israelites would go out to gather twice as much bread to cover the sixth day and the

Sabbath day, since they didn't work on the Sabbath (Exodus 16:1-36).

The Israelites would not have survived without trusting the provision of God and obeying the Word of God to gather their daily portion of bread. Jesus wants us to walk with Him day by day obeying His word and trusting in His provision. He can satisfy all our needs because He is the bread of life and living water.

The fourth verse of the The Lord's Prayer says, "And forgive us our debts, as we also have forgiven our debtors" (Matthew 6:12). Jesus paid our debt in full for the sins we've committed against Him and has forgiven us forever. He reconciled our relationship with the Father through His death, burial, and resurrection. Since we've been forgiven forever through the blood of Jesus, God expects us to forgive others. Jesus warns us that the Father will not forgive us of our offenses if we don't forgive people of their offenses (Matthew 6:15).

When we hold on to an offense committed against us, it becomes a relational debt. Romans 13:8 tell us, "Owe nothing to anyone except to love one another; for the one who loves his neighbor has fulfilled the law." We can't love one another by holding on to a relational debt. Forgiveness releases us from holding onto the debt and can lead to relational reconciliation.

The fifth verse says, "And do not lead us into temptation but deliver us from evil" (Matthew 6:13). Jesus is telling us that God doesn't lead us into temptation, and we need Him to deliver us from Satan. Satan knows the three ways we are tempted and how to influence us to give into the temptation.

If we think we can overcome temptation or the influence of Satan on our own, we are sadly mistaken. First Corinthians 10:12-13 tell us, "Therefore let the one who thinks he stands watch out that he does not fall. No temptation has overtaken you except something common to mankind; and God is faithful, so He will not allow you to be tempted beyond what you are able, but with the temptation will provide the way of escape also, so that you will be able to endure it."

In Matthew 6:32-33, Jesus reminds us of what He said earlier in Matthew 6:8 and adds to it that the Father will provide for our needs. He doesn't promise to provide what we want, but He does promise to provide what we need.

Our demonstration of trust in the Father's provision is to "seek first His Kingdom and His righteousness" (Matthew 6:33) and "do not worry about tomorrow" (Matthew 6:34). When we fail to seek first His Kingdom and His righteousness and start to worry about tomorrow, we demonstrate a lack of trust in the Father. When we do this, we are sinning against God.

In the first few paragraphs of John 16, Jesus warns the disciples of persecution and promises help from the Holy Spirit. He foretells of His death, resurrection, and return to the Father. Then Jesus continues to teach on prayer. He revealed to the disciples (and us) that when we pray, we should pray to the Father in His name. He promises us when we ask for anything in His name, the Father will give it to us.

This verse can easily be taken out of context without an understanding of The Lord's Prayer. What is the "anything" Jesus says we can pray for? To help answer that question, let's look at the second sentence in The Lord's Prayer: "Your Kingdom come. Your will be done, on earth as it is in heaven."

The "anything" we pray for should align with the will of God. The will of God, in other words, is God's plan for His Kingdom. In 1 John 5:14-15, John—the same writer of the Gospel of John—tells us that God only hears what we pray according to His will. We are to pray to the Father according to His will in Jesus' name.

The next question you might ask is, what is the will of God? The will of God is to advance His Kingdom with love. Our responsibility is to love God, love people, make disciples, and glorify God in everything we do. We don't have to have all the answers, and we don't need to know all the details.

You may have another question: What is the specific calling for my life? Pray to the Father, asking the Holy Spirit to lead you in Jesus' name! Then trust God and take a step in the direction He leads you. God already knows what we are going to pray and already has a plan! Now that we have established the model for prayer, we will discuss prayer more in depth including hinderances to prayer, conditions for answered prayer, times of prayer, physical posture in prayer, and kinds of prayer.

Hinderances to Answered Prayer

1. **Praying without knowing God through Jesus**
   John 14:6 – Jesus said, "I am the way, the truth, and the life; no one comes to the Father except through Me."

2. **Disobedience to God's word**
   John 9:31 – "We know that God does not listen to sinners; but if someone is God-fearing and does His will, He listens to Him."

3. **Unconfessed sin**
   Proverbs 28:13 – "One who conceals his wrongdoing will not prosper, but one who confesses and abandons them will find compassion."

4. **An unforgiving attitude**
   Matthew 6:15 – "But if you do not forgive other people, then your Father will not forgive your offenses."

5. **Hatred of godly knowledge and lack of reverence**
   Proverbs 1:28-29 – "Then they will call on me, but I will not answer; they will seek me diligently but will not find me, because they hated knowledge and did not choose the fear of the Lord."

6. **Pride**

   James 4:6 – "But He gives a greater grace. therefore it says, "God is opposed to the proud, but gives grace to the humble.""

7. **Prayers not prayed**

   James 4:2 – "You lust and do not have, so you commit murder. And you are envious and cannot obtain, so you fight and quarrel. You do not have because you do not ask."

8. **Wrong motives**

   James 4:3 – "You ask and do not receive, because you ask with the wrong motives, so that you may spend what you request on your pleasures."

9. **Doubt**

   James 1:6 – "But he must ask in faith without any doubting, for the one who doubts is like the surf of the sea, driven and tossed by the wind."

10. **Double-minded attitude**

    James 1:7-8 – "For that person ought not to expect that he will receive anything from the Lord, being a double-minded man, unstable in all his ways."

11. **Mistreating your spouse**

    1 Peter 3:7 – "You husbands in the same way, live with your wives in an understanding way, as with someone weaker, since she is a woman; and show her honor as a fellow heir of the grace of life, so that your prayers will not be hindered."

12. **Praying for show**

Matthew 6:5 – "And when you pray, you are not to be like the hypocrites; for they love to stand and pray in the synagogues and on the street corners so that they will be seen by people. Truly I say to you, they have their reward in full."

13. **Praying repetitive, empty words**

Matthew 6:7-8 – "And when you are praying, do not use thoughtless repetition as the Gentiles do, for they think that they will be heard because of their many words. So do not be like them; for your Father knows what you need before you ask Him."

Conditions for answered prayer

1. **Pray in secret**

Matthew 6:6 – "But as for you, when you pray, go into your inner room, close your door, and pray to your Father who is in secret; and your Father who sees what is done in secret will reward you."

2. **Pray to the Father**

Matthew 6:9 – "Pray, then, in this way: 'Our Father, who is in heaven, Hallowed be Your Name."

3. **Pray with reverence**

John 9:31 – "We know that God does not listen to sinners; but if someone is God-fearing and does His will, He listens to Him."

4. **Pray with humility**

Luke 18:10-14 – "Two men went up into the temple to pray, one a Pharisee and the other a tax collector. The Pharisee stood and began praying this in regard to himself: 'God, I thank You that I am not like other people: swindlers, crooked, adulterers, or even like this tax collector.

I fast twice a week; I pay tithes of all that I get.' But the tax collector, standing some distance away, was even unwilling to raise his eyes towards heaven, but was beating his chest saying, 'God, be merciful to me, the sinner!'

I tell you, this man went to his house justified rather than the other one; for everyone who exalts himself will be humbled, but the one who humbles himself will be exalted."

5. **Pray confessing sin**
   1 John 1:9 – "If we confess our sins, He is faithful and righteous, so that He will forgive us of our sins and cleanse us from all unrighteousness."

6. **Pray with a forgiving attitude**
   Mark 11:25 – "And whenever you stand praying, forgive, if you have anything against anyone, so that your Father who is in heaven will also forgive your offenses."

7. **Pray in faith**
   Mark 11:24 – "Therefore, I say to you, all things for which you pray and ask, believe that you have received them, and they will be granted to you."

8. **Pray according to God's will**
   1 John 5:14 – "This is the confidence which we have before Him, that, if we ask anything according to His will, He hears us."

9. **Pray from an obedient life**

   John 15:7 – "If you remain in Me, and My words remain in you, ask whatever you wish, and it will be done for you."

10. **Pray from a pure heart**

    2 Timothy 2:22 – "Now flee from youthful lusts and pursue righteousness, faith, love, and peace with those who call on the Lord from a pure heart.

11. **Pray by asking, seeking, knocking**

    Matthew 7:7-11 – "Ask, and it will be given to you; seek, and you will find; knock, and it will be opened to you. For everyone who asks receives, and the one who seeks finds, and to the one who knocks it will be opened. Or what person is there among you who, when his son asks for a loaf of bread, will give him a stone? Or if he asks for a fish, he will not give him a snake, will he? So if you, despite being evil, know how to give good gifts to your children, how much more will your Father who is in heaven give good things to those who ask Him!"

12. **Pray in Jesus' Name**

    John 14:13-14 – "And whatever you ask in My name, this I will do, so that the Father may be glorified in the Son. If you ask Me anything in My name, I will do it."

Times to pray

1. **In the morning**

   Mark 1:35 – "And in the early morning, while it was still dark, Jesus got up, left the house, and went away to a secluded place, and prayed there for a time."

2. **All night**
   Luke 6:12 – "Now it was at this time that He went off to the mountain to pray, and He spent the whole night in prayer with God."

3. **At midnight**
   Acts 16:25 – "Now about midnight Paul and Silas were praying and singing hymns of praise to God, and the prisoners were listening to them."

4. **Continually**
   Ephesians 6:18 – "With every prayer and request, pray at all times in the Spirit, and with this in view, be alert with all perseverance and every request for all the saints."

   1 Thessalonians 5:17 – "Pray without ceasing."

Physical posture of prayer

1. **Falling on one's face**
   Matthew 26:39 – "And He went a little beyond them, and fell on His face and prayed, saying, "My Father, if it is possible, let this cup pass from Me; yet not as I will, but as You will."

2. **Kneeling**
   Luke 22:41 – "And He withdrew from them about a stone's throw, and He knelt down and began to pray."

3. **Standing**
   Mark 11:25 – "And whenever you stand praying, forgive, if you have anything against anyone, so that your Father who is in heaven will also forgive your offenses."

4. **Lifting up hands**

   1 Timothy 2:8 – "Therefore I want the men in every place to pray, lifting up holy hands, without anger and dispute."

Kinds of Prayer

1. **Private**

   Matthew 6:6 – "But as for you, when you pray, go into your inner room, close your door, and pray to your Father who is in secret; and your Father who sees what is done in secret will reward you."

2. **Public**

   Luke 3:21 – "Now when all the people were baptized, Jesus also was baptized, and while He was praying, heaven was opened."

3. **Agreement with others**

   Matthew 18:19-20 – "Again I say to you, that if two of you agree on earth about anything that they may ask, it shall be done for them by My Father who is in heaven. For where two or three have gathered together in My name, I am there in their midst."

4. **Emergency**

   Matthew 14:30 – "But seeing the wind, he became frightened, and when he began to sink, he cried out, saying, "Lord, save me!""

5. **Confession**

   Luke 18:13 – "But the tax collector, standing some distance away, was even unwilling to raise his eyes towards heaven, but was beating his chest saying, 'God, be merciful to me, the sinner!"

6. **Intercession**

   Romans 10:1 – "Brothers and sisters, my heart's desire and my prayer to God for them is for their salvation."

7. **For the Church**

   Colossians 1:3-4 – "We give thanks to God, the Father of our Lord Jesus Christ, praying always for you, since we heard of your faith in Christ Jesus and the love which you have for all the saints."

There's a Prayer for That

In 2009 Apple launched a campaign called "There's and app for that", which promoted that the iPhone has an app for everything. Indeed it was a great marketing campaign, but it didn't compare to the prayers in the Bible for believers to pray. When you search Scripture, you will discover: "There's a prayer for that." However, I encourage you to verify that the prayer you pray aligns with the will of God and is based on the context of the passage of Scripture you read. It's easy to take prayers out of context without understanding the meaning. Remember, the enemy appears as an angel of light to lead us astray from the truth (2 Corinthians 11:14).

Examples of "There's a prayer for that"

1. **Love God with all your heart, soul, and strength**

   Matthew 22:37 – "And He said to him, "You shall love the Lord your God with all your heart, and with all your soul, and with all your mind."

2. **Ask God how you can serve His Kingdom**

    Matthew 6:33 – "Seek first His kingdom and His righteousness, and all these things will be provided to you."

3. **Ask to know Christ more**

    Ephesians 1:17-18 – "That the God of our Lord Jesus Christ, the Father of glory, may give you a spirit of wisdom and of revelation in the knowledge of Him. I pray that the eyes of your heart may be enlightened, so that you will know what is the hope of His calling, what are the riches of the glory of His inheritance in the saints."

4. **Love people the way Jesus loves people**

    John 13:34 – "I am giving you a new commandment, that you love one another; just as I have loved you, that you also love one another."

5. **Increase your capacity to love**

    1 Thessalonians 3:12 – "And may the Lord cause you to increase and overflow in love for one another, and for all people, just as we also do for you."

6. **Glorify God in everything you do**

    Colossians 3:17 – "Whatever you do in word or deed, do everything in the name of the Lord Jesus, giving thanks through Him to God the Father."

7. **Be Spirit led**

    Galatians 5:25 – "If we live by the Spirit, let's follow the Spirit as well."

8. **Grow in the grace and knowledge of Jesus Christ**
   2 Peter 3:18 – "But grow in the grace and the knowledge of our Lord and Savior Jesus Christ. To Him be the glory, both now and to the day of eternity. Amen."

9. **Put on the Lord Jesus Christ**
   Romans 13:14 – "But put on the Lord Jesus Christ, and make no provision for the flesh in regards to its lusts."

10. **Be Strong in the Lord**
    Ephesians 6:10 – "Finally, be strong in the Lord and in the strength of His might."

11. **Put on the full armor of God**
    Ephesians 6:11 – "Put on the full armor of God, so that you will be able to stand firm against the schemes of the devil."

12. **Renew your mind**
    Romans 12:2 – "And do not be conformed to the patterns of this world, but be transformed by the renewing of your mind, so that you may prove what the will of God is, that which is good and acceptable and perfect."

13. **Be quick to hear, slow to speak, and slow to anger**
    James 1:19 – "You know this, my beloved brothers and sisters. Now everyone must be quick to hear, slow to speak, and slow to anger."

14. **Be kind, compassionate, and quick to forgive**
    Ephesians 4:32 – "Be kind to one another, compassionate, forgiving each other, just as God in Christ has also forgiven you."

15. **Walk in a manner worthy of the Lord**
    Colossians 1:9-12 – "For this reason we also, since the day we heard about it, have not ceased praying for you and asking that you may be filled with the knowledge of His will in all spiritual wisdom and understanding, so that you will walk in a manner worthy of the Lord, to please Him in all respects, bearing fruit in every good work and increasing in the knowledge of God; strengthened with all power, according to His glorious might for the attaining of all perseverance and patience; joyously giving thanks to the Father, who has qualified us to share in the inheritance of the saints in light."

16. **Find the way of escape from temptation**
    1 Corinthians 10:13 – "No temptation has overtaken you except something common to mankind; and God is faithful, so He will not allow you to be tempted beyond what you are able, but with the temptation will provide the way of escape also, so that you will be able to endure it."

17. **People in authority**
    1 Timothy 2:1-2 – "First of all, then, I urge that requests, prayers, intercession, and thanksgiving be made in behalf of all people, for kings and all who are in authority, so that we may lead a tranquil and quiet life in all godliness and dignity."

18. **Your enemies**
    Matthew 5:44-45 – "But I say to you, love your enemies and pray for those who persecute you, so that you may prove yourselves to be the sons of your Father who is in heaven; for He causes His sun to rise on the evil and the good, and sends rain on the righteous and the unrighteous."

19. Someone's faith not to fail

Luke 22:32 – "But I have prayed for you, that your faith will not fail; and you, when you have turned back, strengthen your brothers."

20. People that have sinned against you

Acts 7:60 – "Then he fell on his knees and cried out with a loud voice, "Lord, do not hold this sin against them! Having said this, he fell asleep."

21. People in prison

Acts 12:5 – "So Peter was kept in the prison, but prayer for him was being made to God intensely by the church."

22. Reaching people in person

Romans 1:10 – "Always in my prayers requesting if perhaps now, at last by the will of God, I will succeed in coming to you."

23. Boldness to proclaim the Gospel

Ephesians 6:18-19 – "With every prayer and request, pray at all times in the Spirit, and with this in view, be alert with all perseverance and every request for all the saints, and pray in my behalf, that speech may be given to me in the opening of my mouth, to make known with boldness the mystery of the gospel."

24. Opening a closed door to share the Gospel

Colossians 4:3 – "Praying at the same time for us as well, that God will open up to us a door for the word, so that we may proclaim the mystery of Christ, for which I have also been imprisoned."

25. **Equipping people to do God's will**

    Hebrews 13:20-21 – "Now may the God of peace, who brought up from the dead the great Shepherd of the sheep through the blood of the eternal covenant, that is, Jesus our Lord, equip you in every good thing to do His will, working in us that which is pleasing in His sight, through Jesus Christ, to whom be the glory forever and ever. Amen."

26. **Healing sickness and sin**

    James 5:14-16 – "Is anyone among you sick? Then he must call for the elders of the church and they are to pray over him, anointing him with oil in the name of the Lord; and the prayer of faith will restore the one who is sick, and the Lord will raise him up, and if he had committed sins, they will be forgiven him.

    Therefore confess your sins to one another, and pray for one another so that you may be healed. A prayer of a righteous person, when it is brought about, can accomplish much."

Fortress Destroyers

When you think of the word fortress, what comes to mind? Do you think of walls made of stone that protect a city, like the walls of Jericho? Do you think of walls made of stone that protect a country, like the Great Wall of China? What about an ideological fortress like the Iron Curtain? Shortly after World War II, there was an Iron Curtain lifted by the Soviet Union to protect their communist ideology from Western democratic ideology.

Just like there are fortresses that protect cities, countries, and political ideologies, there are spiritual fortresses that keep man bound in darkness. Ever since man rebelled against God in the Garden of Eden, man has hardened his heart towards God and been under the influence of Satan.

Satan is referred to as "the god of this planet" and he has "blinded the minds of the unbelieving so that they will not see the light of the gospel of the glory of Christ, who is the image of God" (2 Corinthians 4:4). Satan is vehemently opposed to the Gospel spreading across planet Earth because he wants to kill, steal, and destroy God's most precious creation—human beings (John 10:10).

Satan wants to prevent people from getting saved, by keeping them in darkness with a hardened heart so they are not receptive to the Gospel. Satan wants to enslave people in major world religions, so they go through the wide gate instead of the narrow gate (Matthew 7:13-14). Satan wants to enslave people in major political systems so that their political party becomes their religion and god. If you think this is limited to communism, think again, because it has already happened in America. Satan wants to enslave people through government systems that control society and prevent the spread of the Gospel. Satan wants to enslave people through ungodly social movements and lifestyles that focus more on what man wants rather than on what God says in His word.

Man is inherently evil and has deceived himself that he is good. Man is in a state of rebellion against God and doesn't think he needs God. Man walks in darkness, blinded by the devil, and doesn't even know it. When you combine the inherent fallen nature of man with the schemes of the devil influencing man, the results are evident throughout the world and throughout history. The entire world is deceived.

When Jesus preached the Gospel on earth, the Jewish religious elite conspired together with the Romans to have Him killed. All the disciples were killed for preaching the Gospel, except for Judas who betrayed Jesus and John who was exiled to the island of Patmos. Preaching the Gospel then and now has a cost. The cost varies generally depending on the country. In Iran, the cost of preaching the Gospel could be prison or death. In America, preaching the Gospel may cost you relationships, your job, business, and, in the future, jail time.

The Gospel is offensive to man because it reveals that the heart of man is wicked, prideful, and in a state of rebellion. Man cannot change his heart because it has been hardened by sin. Man cannot escape the darkness because the light of the Gospel is not in him. The fortress of pride surrounding man's heart and the fortress of deception surrounding man's mind is too powerful to overcome by the flesh: "For though we walk in the flesh, we do not wage battle according to the flesh, for the weapons of our warfare are not of the flesh, but divinely powerful for the destruction of fortresses. We are destroying arguments and all arrogance raised against the knowledge of God, and we are taking every thought captive to the obedience of Christ, and we are ready to punish all disobedience, whenever your obedience is complete" (2 Corinthians 10:3-6).

The weapon of our warfare to destroy fortresses is the Word of God: "For the word of God is living and active, and sharper than any two-edged sword, even penetrating as far as the division of soul and spirit, of both joints and marrow, and able to judge the thoughts and intentions of the heart" (Hebrews 4:12).

The Word of God can penetrate through the fortress of pride surrounding man's heart and the fortress of deception surrounding man's mind. The Word of God declares, "For God so loved the world, that He gave His only Son, so that everyone who believes in Him will not perish but have eternal life. For God did not send the Son into the world to judge the world, but so that the world might be saved through Him" (John 3:16-17).

To advance God's Kingdom with love we must show people the love of God and tell people about the love of God by sharing the Word of God. At times, we are going to offend people and be persecuted for it. If you are a believer, someone showed you the love of God and taught you about the love of God from the Word of God. You responded by faith after hearing the Word of God and being drawn by the Holy Spirit. Romans 10:17 says, "So faith comes from hearing, and hearing by the word of Christ."

The only way for lost people to escape the snare of the devil is to be shown the love of God and taught the love of God from the Word of God so that they can respond by faith.

When a lost person responds by faith and is saved by grace, they come to know the truth and the truth sets them free (John 8:32-36). Jesus is the one who sets lost people free from the snare of the devil.

As believers that have been set free by the truth we still can be led astray by the pride of life, the lust of the flesh, the lust of the eyes, false doctrines, empty chatter, worldly philosophies, politics, nationalism, climate change, ungodly social movements, ungodly lifestyle movements, black helicopter theories, UFO abduction stories, and anything else that becomes more important than God.

Deception starts with thoughts in our minds and feelings in our hearts. Even though we are believers born again by the Spirit, we still have a sinful nature in a human body. We are susceptible to give into deception when we don't stay humble. When we become prideful, thinking that we don't need God, it can develop into a pattern. For example, when we think we don't need God today, then that can lead to tomorrow, the next day, the next day, and so forth.

The more we become disconnected from God the more prone we are to become isolated, which is right where Satan wants us: "Be of sober spirit, be on the alert. Your adversary, the devil, prowls around like a roaring lion, seeking someone to devour. So resist him, firm in your faith, knowing that the same experiences of suffering are being accomplished by your brothers and sisters who are in the world" (1 Peter 5:8-9).

We must stay humble daily, submit to God daily, and resist the devil daily: "But He gives a greater grace. Therefore it says, "God is opposed to the proud, but gives grace to the humble." Submit therefore to God. But resist the devil, and he will flee from you. Come close to God and He will come close to you. Cleanse your hands, you sinners; and purify your hearts, you double-minded" (James 4:6-8).

We must renew our minds daily, destroy arguments and all arrogance raised against the knowledge of God daily, and take every thought captive to the obedience of Christ daily. We must stay connected to the body of Christ through small groups and corporate worship gatherings weekly.

Even when we stay connected to the body of Christ, we must be careful of false prophets that appear in sheep's clothing (Matthew 7:15). False prophets appear to know the truth but are living in deception. They may come up with a new revelation that wasn't previously known or twist Scripture to fit their lifestyle, social movement, or fleshly desires.

The comedian, Jeff Foxworthy, is known for his "Redneck humor" and his famous "You might be a Redneck if" comedy routine. Similar to his "You Might be a Redneck if" routine, I've come up with a "You Can identify a False Prophet if" list so that you can identify false prophets and avoid becoming the laughingstock of Satan. When it comes to false prophets, it's not a laughing matter for the people they deceive.

You can identify a false prophet if they preach sermons without referencing the Word of God.

You can identify a false prophet if they preach sermons from pride, arrogance, or self-righteousness.

You can identify a false prophet if they preach sermons more focused on man's righteous works than the finished work of Jesus Christ.

You can identify a false prophet if they preach sermons more focused on comfort and safety than on trusting and obeying God even when its uncomfortable and dangerous.

You can identify a false prophet if they preach sermons more focused on what man receives for following God's Word, rather than glorifying God for obeying His Word.

You can identify a false prophet if they preach sermons more focused on advancing social movements and lifestyles, rather than advancing God's Kingdom with love.

You can identify a false prophet if they preach sermons more focused on sowing seeds to reap financial rewards, rather than sowing seeds to reap eternal life rewards.

You can identify a false prophet if they preach sermons claiming they have received a new revelation previously unknown.

You can identify a false prophet if they preach sermons claiming that man is a little god because man was created by God.

You can identify a false prophet if they preach sermons claiming you can be "slain in the Spirit."

You can identify a false prophet if they preach sermons

more focused on manifesting the gifts of the Spirit rather than loving your neighbor as yourself.

You can identify a false prophet if they never preach sermons discussing sin, death, or hell.

You can identify a false prophet if they preach sermons that don't point to the death, burial, and resurrection of Jesus Christ as the only way man can be saved.

GOSPEL OFFENSE: CHAPTER 8

Gospel Warfare

The term "guerrilla warfare" stems from the Duke of Wellington's campaigns during the Peninsular War in the 19th century according to Britannica.com. The concept of guerrilla warfare is a type of warfare where a small irregular force attacks a traditional military force with unconventional tactics. This concept has been around since ancient times and is included in the Bible.

In Judges Chapter 2, the generation after Joshua did not know the Lord and started doing evil in the sight of the Lord. They abandoned the Lord and started worshipping the gods of the people who were around them. The Lord's anger burned against the Israelites, and He handed them over to their enemies. Then the Lord raised up judges to save the Israelites from their enemies, yet the people of Israel didn't listen to the judges and fell back into disobedience.

The Lord, moved by compassion, would raise up judges to save the people of Israel from the torment of their captors. Then the judges would die and the people of Israel would become more corrupt. The Lord finally stopped helping the people of Israel to test them for a period to see if they would obey His commandments. However, the people of Israel failed to obey His commands, fell back into slavery, and cried out to the Lord. The Lord was compassionate and responded to their cries by raising up a judge to save the people.

The writer in Hebrews Chapter 11 lists heroic men and women from the Old Testament who answered the call of God including four judges: Gideon, Barak, Jephthah, and Samson. Samson is probably the most well-known person out of those four judges because of the story of Samson and Delilah.

In Judges Chapter 13, the Lord raised up Samson as a judge to deliver the people of Israel from the Philistines. The Lord was with Samson and gave him supernatural strength on the condition that Samson didn't break his covenant with God.

In Judges Chapter 15, Samson caught 300 foxes, lined them up tail to tail, placed a torch in between their tails, then set the torch on fire driving the foxes into the Philistine grain fields to destroy their crops. He also destroyed their vineyards and olive groves. This tactic was unconventional and a demonstration of an ancient guerrilla warfare tactic.

The reason I included this example is to illustrate that God can use what seems to be unconventional tactics to accomplish His Kingdom purpose against impossible odds. It's impossible to think that one man can catch 300 foxes, line them up, and set their tails on fire so that they would run into the grain fields, vineyards, and olive groves. When it comes to God, man aligned with God's will = overcoming impossible odds to fulfill God's will.

When Jesus came to this earth He was surrounded and outnumbered by enemies. Jesus launched His ministry at the age of 30 and used what appeared to be unconventional tactics to advance His Kingdom with love. I call these tactics "Gospel warfare."

The tactics of Jesus were not to force man to change but to draw man to change by speaking the truth in love and demonstrating His lovingkindness. Jesus loved His enemies, turned water into wine, fed the hungry, healed the sick, strengthened the weak, gave grace to the sinner, raised the dead, restored sight to the blind, restored hearing to the mute, cast out demons, confronted the religious elite, gave hope to the hopeless, and boldly proclaimed the truth.

In John Chapter four, Jesus' disciples were baptizing people in Judea and the Pharisees were wanting to stop them, so they returned to Galilee. On the way to Galilee, Jesus had to go through Samaria. Most Jewish people at the time despised Samaritans and even bypassed Samaria by going miles out of the way. Jesus, demonstrating His human nature, had become weary of the long walk and sat down by Jacob's well at noon time. The disciples left Him alone at the well to go into the village to buy some food. Even though Jesus was thirsty, hungry, and tired from the long walk, He intentionally positioned Himself to be at the right place at the right time to meet a Samaritan woman.

The Samaritan woman arrived with her water jug to draw from the well, fill her jug, and satisfy her physical thirst. Jesus engaged with the woman, asking her to give him a drink. She was surprised that Jesus, a Jew by birth, acknowledged her and spoke to her. The woman asked Jesus why He was asking her for a drink. Jesus responded to her by offering her grace, "If you only knew the gift God has for you and who you are speaking to, you would ask me, and I would give you living water" (John 4:10 NLT).

The woman didn't understand what Jesus said to her and asked a few questions. Jesus explained she would never become thirsty again and would have eternal life. This was the first time this woman probably heard someone say something this bold and unconventional. She was excited and asked to receive this water. Instead of Jesus giving her the water immediately, He tells her to go and get her husband. She told Jesus she didn't have a husband.

Jesus agreed with her and told her she had five husbands and was currently shacked up with a man. It was obvious the woman had been brokenhearted and Jesus was there demonstrating, "The Lord is near to the brokenhearted and saves those who are crushed in spirit" (Psalm 34:18).

She shifted the conversation away from her failures and acknowledged that Jesus was a prophet and asked why Jews insisted that Jerusalem is the only place or "conventional way" to worship God. Jesus explained to her that the time is coming for the "conventional way" of worshipping God to change, that Jews would no longer be the only ones that know all about God, and that salvation comes from the Jews.

Jesus repeated the point that the time is coming. Then He revealed that the time is here, now, when true worshippers will worship the Father in Spirit and truth. The conventional way of worshipping God immediately changed from that day forward and all people could worship God anywhere, anytime, and anyplace. The woman told Jesus she knew the Messiah was coming and that He would explain everything. Then Jesus told her, "I am He, the One speaking to you" (John 4:26).

Can you imagine what the Samaritan woman was thinking and feeling? She had been brokenhearted, going through five failed marriages and probably was hesitant to remarry, which is why she was shacked up with a man. She had no idea that marriage was a foreshadow of the marriage between the Messiah and His Church—a marriage that will never end by divorce or death.

When the disciples returned from the village, they saw Jesus talking to the Samaritan woman and were shocked. Then the woman left her jug at the well and ran back to the village testifying about her encounter with Jesus. Can you imagine what the village people were thinking? They probably knew all about her five failed marriages and being shacked up with a man. Now she reported she might have met the Messiah! I'm confident these village people weren't thinking "It's fun to stay at the YMCA" because they came streaming from the village to meet Jesus.

God used an unconventional method—Jesus a Jewish man speaking to a Samaritan woman—to reach a broken person by breaking through cultural boundaries. God used an unconventional person, the Samaritan woman, to announce the arrival of the Messiah.

The world has defined "church" as the building for public Christian worship as to limit what is conventionally acceptable in society. The Bible says believers are members of the body of Christ (1 Corinthians 12:27) and the body of Christ is the Church (Ephesians 5:23). We are a temple of the Holy Spirit (1 Corinthians 6:19) and worship the Father in Spirit and in truth (John 4:23). We are to live our lives as a living and holy sacrifice, not conformed to the behaviors and customs of this world (Romans 12:1-2). In short, we are the Church everywhere we go, and we worship God in everything we do. The behaviors and customs we demonstrate to the world are unconventional because we are advancing God's Kingdom with love.

When Jesus lived on this earth, He was intentional to build relationships and engage with people right where they were. He used methods that were unconventional in the world, but intentional, to demonstrate His lovingkindness and forgiveness. He spoke the truth in love, fearless of the consequences by the world. He transformed a group of unqualified men behind enemy lines into a special forces squad led and empowered by the Holy Spirit.

Over 2000 years later, He continues to multiply His Kingdom through the process of saving people by grace through faith and transforming unqualified people into special forces troops behind enemy lines to do greater things than what Jesus did on this earth (John 14:12). Yes, Jesus says we will do the works He did and even greater works. Why did He say that?....easy.... The Spirit who raised Christ from the dead lives in us. He is the Holy Spirit, and He is God. When Jesus was on the earth, He ministered to a small geographic region, and the Holy Spirit was not sent to all believers yet. Since the day of Pentecost, recorded in the book of Acts, the Holy Spirit was sent and dwells in all believers.

The influence of Jesus has spread from a small geographic region to the entire world. In short, He has a global army that the gates of hell cannot prevail against (Matthew 16:18).

When I think about greater things, I start to think about doing "big things" to advance God's Kingdom with love, but there are two principles to learn. The fruit flows from the vine so that God is glorified (John 15:1), and we must be faithful in the small things before God will trust us with bigger things (Luke 16:10).

When a branch on a vine starts growing it has a small footprint and produces small fruit. As the branch continues to grow through the vine the footprint of the branch increases, and more fruit is produced. If the vine doesn't cause the growth, then the branch doesn't grow. Jesus is the vine, and we are the branch. He wants us to bear much fruit through Him, and He will prune us if we are not bearing fruit (John 15:2).

The small things in our life start with loving our neighbor as ourself, which is the entire law summed up in Galatians 5:14. As the love of God increases in our lives, the fruit will increase in our lives. Jesus said that His disciples will be known for how we love, not what greater things we do. The things we do should be an outflow of the love of God so people are drawn to God, and God is glorified.

SECTION 3
Gospel Victory

GOSPEL OFFENSE: CHAPTER 9

The Final Battles

When I look at the American flag, the red reminds me of the blood that was shed that gave me the freedom to write this book. I'm thankful for the men and women who have served in our armed forces and sacrificed for our country.

When I think about the cross, I'm reminded of the blood Jesus shed to set me free from the bondage of sin, the snare of the devil, and death. I'm thankful for the Father sending Jesus to die for my sins and the Holy Spirit raising Jesus from the dead.

In the book of Revelation, there will be two periods of time where Satan will operate unrestrained. There will be bloodshed the likes of which the world has never seen and two final battles on a scale the world has never seen.

The Tribulation Battle

The first period when Satan will be allowed to operate unrestrained is known as the tribulation. During the tribulation period the world will experience a series of judgements from God and be under the influence of Satan (the dragon), the beast, and the false prophet. At the end of this period, Satan (the dragon), the beast, and the false prophet will gather the kings of the earth and their armies to wage war against the Lamb.

In Revelation 19:11-16, Jesus the Lamb returns as a Great Warrior King with His Great Army: "And I saw heaven opened, and behold, a white horse, and He who sat on it is called Faithful and True, and in righteousness He judges and wages war. His eyes are a flame of fire, and on His head are many crowns; and He has a name written on Him which no one knows except Himself. He is clothed with a robe dipped in blood, and His name is called The Word of God. And the armies which are in heaven, clothed in fine linen, white and clean, were following Him on white horses.

From His mouth comes a sharp sword, so that with it He may strike down the nations, and He will rule them with a rod of iron; and He treads the wine press of the fierce wrath of God, the Almighty. And on His robe and on His thigh He has a name written; "KING OF KINGS, AND LORD OR LORDS."

In Revelation 19:17-19, an angel cries out to all the birds that fly in midheaven to assemble for a great feast as the beast and the kings of the earth assemble to war against Jesus. The scary part about this is that the kings of the earth and their armies are so deceived they still fight against Jesus who appears out of heaven with His great army.

If you are wondering what happens next, listen to the chorus of the song *Bodies* by Drowning Pool. The chorus says, "Let the bodies hit the floor." In Revelation 19:20-21, the beast and false prophet are seized and thrown into the lake of fire. Then the rest of the kings of the earth and their armies are killed with the sword that comes out of the mouth of Jesus and all the birds are filled with their flesh.

The Millennial Reign Battle

In Revelation 20, Satan is bound with a great chain for one thousand years in the abyss. The people who were beheaded for the testimony of Jesus, who didn't worship the beast or his image and didn't receive the mark of the beast during the tribulation, are resurrected and reign with Jesus for one thousand years.

At the end of the one-thousand-year reign Satan is released from the abyss and is given one last chance to deceive the nations. Satan gathers up an army like the sand of the seashore to surround the beloved city filled with God's people. This time fire comes down from heaven and devours the entire army. Satan is thrown into the lake of fire and brimstone to be punished for eternity. I wonder if we will take a praise break in heaven after this happens to sing, "Na na na na, na na na na, hey hey hey, goodbye!"

The Great White Throne Judgement

At the conclusion of the final battle a great white throne will appear with Jesus sitting on it. The dead, great and small, will stand before the throne. The books will be opened, and another book will be opened. The "books" contain the deeds written down of each dead person, and the book of life contains the names of the people that are saved. Notice the term "books" is used for the people who are going to the lake of fire, and there is only one book of life that is used for people who are saved. This means more people will be thrown into the lake of fire than will be saved.

Ultimately, the lake of fire isn't going to scare anyone into being saved because it's the kindness of God that leads people to repentance (Romans 2:4). The most important question you can ask yourself is, are you 100% certain your name is written in the book of life?

If you are not 100% certain your name is written in the book of life, you can respond to the kindness of God right now by confessing with your mouth Jesus as Lord and believing in your heart God raised Him from the dead (Romans 10:9). You will be saved, and your name will be written in the book of life.

BRIAN BENTON

The New Creation

For us who have our names written in the book of life, we will live with God forever as described in Revelation Chapters 21 and 22.

In Revelation 21, God creates a new heaven, a new earth, and a new Jerusalem where He will dwell among His people. He will wipe away every tear from our eyes. There will no longer be any death. There will no longer be any mourning, crying, or pain. The first things will have passed away.

In Revelation 22, the throne of God and of the Lamb is in the middle of a street, and on each side of the throne is the tree of life that bears twelve kinds of fruit every month, and the leaves of the tree will heal the nations.

In the Garden of Eden there was the tree of the knowledge of good and evil and the tree of life. The tree of the knowledge of good and evil was in the middle of the garden. In the Garden of Eden, man had the ability to choose to eat from the tree of the knowledge of good and evil or eat from the tree of life. In the new creation, the throne of God and of the Lamb is in the middle of a street between a tree of life on each side.

In the new creation, we will not be able to choose evil because evil will no longer exist. In the new creation, we will live forever because death will no longer exist. In the new creation, we will no longer live under a curse because the curse will no longer exist. In the new creation, we will no longer need the sun because the Lord God will illuminate us. In the new creation, we will reign with God forever and ever. Amen!

GOSPEL OFFENSE: CHAPTER 10

The Final Analysis

The time we live on planet Earth is short, and the opportunity to advance God's kingdom with love is now and until we are promoted to glory. This is not the time to play defense. It is the time to go on offense with the Gospel. The Gospel is the Good News that Jesus Christ defeated Satan, overcame the world, died for our sins, and conquered death.

We go on offense by courageously following our Great Warrior King, Jesus Christ, in battle to advance God's kingdom with love. We advance God's kingdom by loving God, loving people, making disciples, and glorifying God in everything we do.

Now go advance God's Kingdom with love!

Printed in the United States
by Baker & Taylor Publisher Services